CHEATING
DEATH
TWICE

CONFESSIONS OF A SOLDIER

MICHAEL PAGE

CHEATING DEATH TWICE

CONFESSIONS OF A SOLDIER

MEREO
Cirencester

Published by Mereo

Mereo is an imprint of Memoirs Publishing

25 Market Place, Cirencester, Gloucestershire GL7 2NX
Tel: 01285 640485, Email: info@mereobooks.com
www.memoirspublishing.com, www.mereobooks.com

ISBN: 978-1-909544-79-6

ACKNOWLEDGEMENTS

I wish to thank my wife and family for their constant support and encouragement whilst I worked on my story; they all believed in me even when I lost faith. Also, a big thank you to Charles Muller at Diadem Books for making my dream come true.

TO COIN A PHRASE

Do not think of me as being any kind of fool, a philistine or a wannabe one-day famous philosopher. I say that I can remember my previous lives because it is true. I can remember them now, and always have done so.

Now after many years of trying to unravel the sounds and the strange images in my head as well as coming to terms with the residual emotions, I say that I have unravelled secrets and now realise that I have also remembered actually being conceived in my mother's womb... This is no fantasy! I believe that it is a very important statement that should be considered very carefully because there will always be ramifications, and I am ready now even to be cross-examined.

I dream at night when I sleep, yes often, and I have been known to fantasise, but believe me when I say that I have never dreamt of, or ever fantasised about being cold, hungry, wet, unwashed, having fleas in my hair, being shouted at, or of being scared for my life with my body trembling with fear. Fantasies and dreams are not memories! Fantasies and dreams are often delightfully uncontrollable, yet comfortable, enjoyable and for me at least often very erotic whereas memories can be very painful.

To coin a phrase...

However, our actual human memories are real things you know both inside and out; you can taste them on your tongue and you can remember the smell of them because they are really inside your head; in your mind you can rewind memories straight back to the beginning or stop in the middle and fast forward if you like, and every bit is always exactly the same as the last time....

FOREWORD

This book was going to be called *Whispering Grass* but I decided instead to call it what it is rather than have a romantic title that no-one would ever understand. So this book is called... *Cheating Death Twice: The confessions of a soldier...*

The thing is, I have always remembered these previous lives. However, being born and bred in England some time after the Second World War, it has not been very easy for me to talk about what I remember from before my birth. Religious dogma made sure that my parents and my immediate society did not believe in such things. Luckily for me though, it is in my nature to want to work things out, to explain how things can be connected, and I do not give up very easily. But it has taken me a very long time to work out just how you can experience different lives—again and again.

There has been much soul searching done throughout all of my life, as some of my memories were very hard to understand; it was like some memories were encrypted. Memories of secrets perhaps, or should I say that I had memories inside of my head of things previous to this book—the Doors of Heaven and The book of Life memories that I could not understand. It seems to me now though, that these memories could only be correctly unlocked and understood through learning about our own natural biological functions of reproduction, including our actual conception through copulation, pregnancy and child birth. The only logical explanation that I could come to is that mankind has either been created by God, or cross bred, many thousands of years ago by some other type of advanced Beings leaving us with an immortal soul which itself enjoys a continual sense of awareness...

Nothing is ever done without a reason, and the only reason I can imagine that some Ancient Gods would have to tamper with our physiological and psychological structure would have to have been to deliberately create a detachable mind in humans—that is, detachable from the normal restraints of animal function and focus, i.e. mental focus on immediate physical needs—and as such, different from that of any of our animal counterparts...

If the focus of the mind can detach from the instinctive animal needs of the body, then we can use our minds for many different and diverse projects... Thus, this very unusual detachable mind might have the side effect of being able to survive the physical death and at some time reincarnate into another body... And, if your mind, soul or psyche can survive outside of any physical realm, then it needs some power source other than flesh and nutrients brought through a blood supply. This power has been identified as having an electrical base (cf. the EEG Machine—Electroencephalography). There are electrical and magnetic forces all around this world and running right through us. So my theory about the human mind and what force powers it, so far, has a scientific basis.

Thus, if our thinking minds, our souls or our psyche (whichever name you wish to apply to it) has an ability to have continuous self-awareness, then would it not be possible to remember being conceived and remember being born? This is what I believe I have experienced, for these are the things that I remember...

Obviously I might be wrong about all of this, and that is okay with me. I would much rather tell the world what I seem to be able to remember, rather than keep it to myself and pretend that 'this kind of thing' cannot ever happen. So why then am I bothering to write about this subject, if I might have made a mistake? The answer is, of course, because if I am right in the fact that I do remember these things, and if I am right in my understanding of how it works, then what I know will be very important to our understanding of spirituality.

So, do not take this book as any ordinarily imagined tale or some kind of fictional story, not by any account. This is my testimony of my memories of previous lives, and of my memory of actually reincarnating back into this life, whereby I can even remember coming together in the womb and being born again. This is a testament of my belief in the continuous or perpetual self-awareness of the soul...

Cheating Death naturally follows on from *The Three Lives of Peter Miller* which contains all of my past life memories, of being alive and of being dead. Even more amazingly, as I understand it now, I have my own memories of actually being conceived into this life. (Yes; when male spermatozoa delivers its genetic memory on coded DNA strands and fertilizes the female egg.) And here I continue with further revelations and discussion about these strange memories within my own mind that I have been trying to unravel for all of my adult life...

...Now in my ageing years (52 now), I think that I can just about understand how it can be possible to Cheat Death, spurn the grim reaper and live on through life after life! I believe that anyone can do this, just through understanding the mechanisms behind it in life. It is not anything to do with who we are, or who we once were, and I do not believe it to be in any way supernatural.

Here I confess to have been hiding a secret for many years, but now I feel old enough to come out of the closest and tell it straight to all and sundry. Being born into this life in our modern World, complete with memories of previous lives once lived far away from here in other countries, is one thing which plays tricks with our personal perspective of life and death...

Being born in the English Countryside straight after the Second World War and as a child confessing to having been a German Soldier in a former life during the First World War and fighting on the western front (First World War, complete with my black pointed metal helmet, I need to add), was at the very least frowned upon, and not in the least bit advantageous to being treated well, loved or treasured by my very Victorian natured (English) parents. My father had lost an older brother to the Second World War and he was not pleased at all with my opening statement...

But then, in this life, in my life as an adult, also having *an out-of-the-body experience* is cold-blooded confirmation that your inner spirit can, and will survive outside-of-the-body quite happily, quite independently, without any solid or material physical form...

So now after many years of concentration, deliberation and pondering on this subject, I do now solidly declare that I was once a sailor on a Portuguese Sailing Ship and later on in another continuing life awareness, I served as a Soldier in the First World War, after being shot dead, remembering what it feels like mentally to be dead and here, in my confessions of a dead soldier, I freely admit it, and will try to explain just how it does happen...

Here and now I will try to share my understanding of the Human Mind! Unique in this entire world, yes, but I question how exactly it works, asking what exactly it is made of. And where exactly is it?

One important question for any student of the concept of immortality to consider is this: is your thinking, reasoning and calculating mind actually what the Holy Scriptures refer to as your *spiritual soul*?

And if it is a Spiritual Soul, shouldn't it naturally survive mortal death and be allowed to continue on its journey through time? What force powers the mind? How is it related to the physical body, and is it that solidly connected to the physical world? And can your Soul transmigrate?

Whilst trying to behave like a normal person, I am also endeavouring to learn about my chosen occupation in construction, study some philosophy, keep my job and raise a family. I have also been trying to work out how we can remember previous lives and how anyone can remember being dead!

Now I have lived my life without criticism and now that my previous embarrassment has gone, I will not mind if my understandings are found to be erroneous, and I do not mind if some people dismiss my story as pure fantasy. However, I have had these memories in my head all of my life, and as I cannot come up with any other possible explanation of why they are in my head, I will just have to assume that I am right.

And if I am right, then what I have to say will become very important evidence that the soul is a timeless form and has a continual stream of self-awareness. (We are, in other words, immortal.)

…So here in *Cheating Death* I very willingly share my thoughts on the subject with you.

        ★   ★   ★

This book is not a fantasy, as I confessed well over one year ago when I wrote *The Three Lives of Peter Miller*. I really do have these memories of past lives. Therefore, this is not a book like any other published before. So it doesn't have to be big, and it doesn't have to flow from chapter to chapter as it's more like a witness's statement of an important event, a rolling confession even, than a chronological or progressive argument. I don't mind repeating myself several times, chapter after chapter, and I have to compare my beliefs to the Ancient Egyptian beliefs about the spirit world and make some comments upon Sigmund Freud's description of the layers of the mind. I am trying here to present a sort of testament of the actual existence of the immortal-human-soul.

Sceptics will obviously dismiss this as made up garbage. However, my memories prove to me anyway, that we do have a continuous or perpetual-self-awareness throughout all of time. Death of the mortal flesh will not stop it. It is like a 'mind mechanism' if you like, that needs to be presented to the reader in many, various and diverse ways. So it's going to be more like a technical book examining methods, motives and mysteries in different ways. In the final chapters I am going to agree with some principles from Ancient Egyptian Mythology which are amazingly similar to Sigmund Freud's understanding of the human mind where the Egyptians and Freud seem to agree that the mind is made up of three types of layers. The **id**, which is present at birth and the immortal soul, the second layer being the **ego**, which is hunger, lust, and greed, which comes into existence through earthly desires; and the **super ego**, which develops through maturity and logic. I am also going to state categorically that there is a forth layer of the human mind, and that being the **rise of the id**, which, after being repressed by the ego and the super ego because of the forces of natural needs, the rise of the **id** spirit develops in later life, and this is where the id tries to express itself, perhaps through what is now called in mankind, the mid-life-crisis!

CHAPTER ONE

Who told Albert Einstein (1879-1955) to spend his life searching for relativity? Why did Isaac Newton (1642-1727) want to become a physicist? And how exactly did Louis Pasteur (1822-1895) discover Penicillin?

Throughout all of mankind's history on this Earth, it appears that there has always been a small percentage of the population whose only ambition in life seems to have been set in stone, right from the day of their birth to explore the world for real knowledge of the past, the truth about the universe, and to search for real understanding of our human origins. Explorers always search the earth for the lost treasures of the Ancient World, and the philosophers seek for the real meaning of life in this mysterious universe. So I ask, how is it that these few people seem to know as an absolute fact, from the moment of birth, that there is *more truth* to be found, and more answers to questions? Are these people perhaps continuing their search for the truth, life after life, rather than just starting out afresh? And if not, how do they find their path in life so early on?

Over these years it has slowly dawned upon me that some few people on earth really do know they have a set destiny from the moment they are born—destinies that are like difficult tasks which they are expected to work on and succeed in. Destinies, set by whom? And for what purpose? To help mankind perhaps, or to make further progress in our understanding of ourselves? But why? Ancient texts suggest that these tasks seem to have been given out by the gods, but then, to whom—only to the worthy and to the brave? How can this be true? Are we not each of us born 'brand new' into this world with equal opportunities?

There are **geologists** who seek the knowledge about the age and structure of our Earth. There are the **archaeologists** who excavate the remains of our most Ancient Civilizations and continually strive to understand the nature of their past existence and recover their artefacts and lost knowledge, and the **chemists** who research the nature of obscure substances. There have also been the **theologians,** the scholars of Religion who seek to understand the mysterious ways of God and the nature of the Heavens. There are the **mathematicians** who break down everything into formulae, equations and fractions. And now we have the **scientists** who are convinced that 'the solid matter of earth' has an equal and an opposite form, Black Matter, invisible matter … and anti-matter or at the sub-atomic-level… regarded as the God particle!

The opposite of matter, a powerful binding force, ever present and yet it is undetectable by our senses and invisible to the naked eye; yet scientists continue to search for it, to find it, to explain it and they most probably intend to use it, or exploit it, again most probably with the intention of providing the power for something like a spacecraft's hyper-drive engine.

But then by a strange coincidence, at the very same time there are many other people, in fact many millions of people, who belong to any one of the many established world religions, who have always believed in, and still do believe in and probably will always believe in, the existence of **God** and the **Holy Ghost**—an equally powerful binding life force, ever present and yet undetectable by our senses and invisible to the naked eye. It's a delicious irony, a witticism perhaps, or is any similarity unimportant? Another thing for a student of immortality to question is the very nature of the human mind, how it works, what force powers it and to question its relation to the physical body...

The mind-body question has been debated by many great thinkers from all the ages because it is a philosophical question. And like many questions, the mind-body question arises only when we try to explain in words how we understand the way something works or how this strange thing even exists, with any degree of human logic.

Human mental experience in its normal waking function consists of a self-conscious awareness of different kinds of phenomena, which philosophers apparently refer to as mental contents. Mental contents are just the sort of things we are ordinarily aware of in daily life, such as wind and rain, hot and cold, a working day or a day off, and ordinary everyday desire for food, refreshment and, of course, our aches and pains—and many such like sensations which tell us about the nature of the physical world around us through our senses, such as sight, sounds, smells, tastes and through the skin with the sensation of touch.

There are also our internal bodily sensations that inform us of our own physical well-being, from being cold or hot or shivery to feelings of pleasure through to many levels of illness or to the many minor irritations and severe pain. We are also constantly aware of the state of our emotional life, via consciousness of our own moods and our often, roller-coaster emotions. These fluctuate more in some people than others, as do our sensations that are experienced to a greater or lesser degree depending on our current circumstances, and over rather longer periods, from hours, days, stretching into years, all of which contribute to that mysterious condition we call happiness or contentment.

Then it seems that we are also continually aware of our own inner thoughts; we have our unlearnt common sense, individual beliefs, genetic memory, our unique opinions, wishes, desires, personal life goals, faiths, fantasies and personal needs, which, again are subject to development and change over time.

And then you have memories. A human being is a natural recorder of events. This ability is essential and one of the core things that distinguishes us as humans. We naturally remember, in varying degrees of vividness, detail and accuracy, all of the events and experiences of our lives, which we need to store away carefully because our memories, both individual or combined, are needed for every other mental process that we can ever make... You would never develop a personality without a memory and you would find it very hard to make any decision, or have any opinion about anything, without a memory; you could not even desire to do something or to eat something in particular without having this background pool of memories!

And we have our unique imaginings and fantasies. We can imagine things and other situations which have not happened to us; we can imagine people in faraway places, the like of which we have never met in life. Inventors and architects can imagine complicated engines and superstructures the like of which the world has never seen. Who first imagined the flying machine, a submarine or hydro-electric power plants? These imaginings or fantasies can be more or less vivid, long and drawn out, or, in a moment's distraction, are quickly dissipated.

We use our fantasies and our imaginings to gather ideas about what we think we need, or to work out what we desire most from this life and things that will benefit our future, or as in a sexual fantasy, for the relief of a certain tension. What I am saying here is, I know that my memories of former lives are real; my memories are not born of dreams or of fantasies, and I have something else to offer, because it seems to be a matter of fact that **I also remember being dead.**

That is, I remember being able to think for myself between lives—thinking, reasoning, even arguing with myself about the true nature of the human mind and our world.

You will have to study every word of what I am saying before you can even begin to judge for yourself if we all have a continuous sense of awareness; or, in my case, that, a very long time ago, when I was just a small child, or even before then, perhaps right at my very birth, my mind, for no apparent reason at all, imagined these previous lives and imagined what it must feel like **to be a dead German soldier!**

Our world is a very confusing place indeed, not yet fully understood, and still very full of wonderful things and real mysteries to ponder on. So it is not an easy task to write about our world, describe mythological ancient gods, the supernatural, reveal the secrets of the spiritual world and magical journeys through the underworld where evil lurks at every turn, with any amount of conviction without some actual experience of it.

I do not believe for a moment that you can just sit down and start writing about these mysteries; you cannot just speculate or imagine their complexities or assume to understand the rules or the function of the unimaginable. However, the spirit world must exist, not in any distant or other parallel dimension, but right here on this earth; perhaps the spirit world flows right beneath our feet, flowing all around our ankles and perhaps, eventually, along its slow winding journey it ultimately disappears deep into the bowls of the Earth.

Many stories exist about this fantastical other world, where the **spirits of the dead roam**, where they do battle with dreadful demons and desperately try to find safe passage back to a new mortal life. Why have people of every nation imagined and tried to describe this other world? All of this magic and mystery must surround us constantly, but most cannot see it, let alone understand it, as its mechanisms are far beyond our mortal realms of comprehension.

However, all puzzles can be put together if you have the time and all of the pieces. That said, it appears to me that thousands of years ago the people of the Ancient World knew all about the power of the human mind, the Supernatural and the Spiritual World, and that they did not just understand it but also tried very hard to manipulate it with the sole desire of cheating death, and then made up their colourful stories around their understanding to perpetuate their real knowledge through time and on into the future.

Yes, I believe that I can now explain how it works and what powers it, and yes, I could be mistaken, but my point is, and I have always thought this, what if I am right?

I believe with every single molecule of my body that I am correct in my memories and in my understanding of the continuous awareness of the soul after physical death. So writing about the subject of the supernatural abilities of the human mind today takes a lot of courage unless you have some of the pieces of this puzzle to share with the world at large!

So, obviously I believe that I do have a piece of this **supernatural puzzle** that I wish to share with you today. I am going to put it forward as evidence that the spirit world exists, even though some people will quite naturally, instantly dismiss my evidence and just imagine it to be false or pure fantasy. Others, I hope, will treasure these—my—revelations within their hearts and minds forever and a day...

My great interest in the subject of the Underworld, Ancient

Greek Gods and Spiritual forms was born with me into this life; it is part of my personality that has lived before and has not been forced upon me by anything or anyone in this life; somehow, it came through with me from the other side.

Yes, I remember my previous lives and I can remember a whole lot more besides. I believe that I can remember exactly what it feels like (mentally aware) to be dead, and no, that is not a contradiction in terms. So no, I will say that I remember my mind being active and of being very conscious of my body being lifeless; that would be a far more accurate statement! And after being dead for a long time, (about forty-four years or so I would have to guess), I believe that I can even remember being conceived in the womb and being carried for nine months to full term.

...And, if I am correct about all of this, I will be the very first person ever to write about remembering the actual experience of the surviving soul, extant within a human embryonic sack (female ovum) being fertilized, receiving DNA and being a self-aware growing foetus and remembering developing inside of the womb and actually being able to see nutrients flowing through the umbilical cord!

It's really amazing I know, but again, if I am right, my revelations here will have a great deal of impact upon the way we understand our world, understand ourselves, and help us understand what we are capable of and highlight the glory of our spirituality...

So, is my ability to remember these things a real gift from the gods? Am I unique? Is it just my imagination going into overdrive? Or is this book really going to be one of the most important books about the extraordinary abilities of the human mind that the world has ever known...?

But then, there are other more scholarly ways of explaining this! My memory might perform perfectly naturally and not be any such supernatural gift. On a physiological level perhaps my own personal theory of our natural-supernatural abilities relating to human memory function and memory storage was accidentally revealed to me on a day in 1987 when I fell off a ladder.

On this day I was doing a really stupid thing. Back then I had no training in Health and Safety at work issues or requirements and I fell off of a ladder and I crashed to the ground onto my back in to the middle of a road and had my only **out-of-the body-experience** to date. That was when I learned for an actual fact that my spiritual inner being and my (and your) spiritual self, my soul and your soul, my digital sub-atomic-memory and your digital sub-atomic memory, can exist outside-of the mortal body. I was floating in the air perfectly intact with all of my memories and complete with my modern identity, individuality and personality.

In this book, I want to talk about and question, why I have inside of my own head, memories of several previous lives, memories of life and of death, dating back for a very long time! I need to put forward the question: how can someone remember being dead? And the question: how can someone even remember being conceived?

I also remember keeping watch over the ocean waves from a crow's nest high up on the top of a mast on a sailing ship, of falling from the rigging of this tall ship and drowning at sea and then, in another life, being a young man serving as a Prussian Soldier (complete with metal pointy hat) in the very wet and muddy front line trenches of the First World War.

Believing in the immortal soul and in Reincarnation is not just my story. Many classical thinkers made reference to the belief in the immortal soul—writers such as Homer, Plato and Euripides.

If I am remembering accurately, then my own spiritual journey from my last life to being born into this life, took perhaps a little less than fifty earth years, and was obviously not by the longest or by the hardest route. Luckily for me, I believe that I met or interacted with a spiritual guide, the spirit of a very clever man who I choose to call 'Michael Faraday'.

When I was dead on the other side, my spirit guide willingly and deliberately helped me to find my salvation and gave me perhaps supernatural information to help me on to my one true path... And all that has happened to me, and all that I have discovered about the spirit world and all I have come to understand about the Underworld, I now share with you.

CHAPTER TWO

Opening of the mouth and revealing the words of truth.
Okay, so you've found me out! I'm not a real fiction writer, or
at least that was never my real intention, and so this is not a
fairy tale. To my mind I am just an ordinary working man. I
am in the building trade and have always been employed in
construction, working as a Civil Engineer now, but other than
that, I am just an ordinary human being, married with my own
children. And if you can forgive me for just being some
ordinary fellow, then I will begin to take one great big leap of
faith and admit that my story, incredibly, is about the immortal
soul, my previous lives and intricate details of being conceived
in my mother's womb and of being born again...

This is no fictional tale, this is my Real Story, a Testimony of
my previous existence if you like, and I want it to be seen as
evidence of my belief that we have a continuous and everlasting
self-awareness of experience. Something tells me this is the
right time now to tell it; that means just in case I have any more
accidents concerning the connection of metal Road Pins and
High Voltage electric cables! So I must say that, for many
mysterious and magical reasons, I have always remembered
previous lives!

I remember drowning in the sea which really was not very nice and I remember serving as a soldier in the trenches of the First World War. In fact, I believe that I have experienced many previous lives and now I understand that it can happen to all of us! It might have taken me a while to understand it, pondering and postulating on difficult questions concerning the earth's mechanisms, magnetisms and electrical forces which, combined, allows for reincarnation of the soul to take place whilst also dealing with other people's *negativity* which is often infuriating. But now I think that I do know how it can happen! And it is not through some magical force, no gift from the gods or by being anything other-worldly that has allowed me to come back to this life.

...No, I believe that it is a completely natural process for any **human-being to continually exist.** However, there seems to be just one simple rule: at the very moment of your death, you do have to believe in it... to carry the knowledge over!

I was born here in 1961 and my upbringing, sadly, was not conducive (not contributing or causative of my thoughts) or favouring of my pre-'this life' memories. So I tried to hide them right out of sight, right at the back of my conscious mind.

However, when I was at my secondary school in the early eighties, my English teacher, a certain Mr Branch, one day asked us all in his class, if anyone of us knew any fascinating facts about this world in which we lived, and, if any pupil did know something, then, he or she would have the chance to give the rest of the class a talk about this one subject or this special thing.

I was about **thirteen years** old at that time. I struggled to think, but as hard as I tried, I did not seem to know anything at all about our world; nothing, that is, that I would ever dare to say out loud!

But I did know something! I knew quite a lot really, but it was all old stuff about borders, papers, black mountains, machine guns and barbed wire from before.

Somehow it was all coming straight back to me from a previous time, from a previous life experience. And the more I tried to think of something about this life to impress our teacher, the more rattling of machine guns and the more screaming from dying men, that I could hear from inside of my head. But I dared not mention any of this to a class full of horrid children, not to Mr Branch or any other mortal being for that matter!

...Though, looking back on that time, I did know some things. I knew what a Philistine was, I knew what a Pharaoh was, what a Sarcophagus was, and what a Semite was. I thought for some strange reason that my real name was, or is, **Prometheus,** depending on your perspective (your position, view or orientation). I knew for a fact that a sarcophagus actually contained a bound and prepared mummy that was literally **the mother of an immortal soul**, and I knew exactly what it feels like to be lying in a field dead!

...These things I had swirling around in my head because somehow, long before I was born here into this life, I had died and passed over into the spirit world.

But with some help I found my way through the white mists of time and through the huge creaking doors of the Temple of the Gods and I had gazed in awe upon the white Book of Life where lines of code where being revealed right in front of me!

However, back then, I was far too young, far too confused and far too embarrassed ever to speak of these strange things; I could never have explained it to anybody anyway. How could a child explain what it really feels like to be dead, to explain just how the spirit world works, tell the world about the 'Book of Life' with all its hidden information about people's future lives. There's no way; even my own biological parents thought me to be more than a little bit crazy!

After many years of actually being haunted by these memories, I decided to start trying to work them out, like it was a huge puzzle that could be pieced together. Deciding what was a dream and what constituted a memory was my very first mental task. It was difficult at times because your dreams are, at times, full of your memories; however, I came to understand that a dream is something you sometimes remember having in the first minutes after waking in the morning. Perhaps still with 'sleep in your eyes' you can sometimes try to hang on to the very last moments of a pleasurable experience that you have absolutely no control over, no control over whatsoever, and it slips away, back down into the **playground of your sub-conscious mind…**

By the same token, a fantasy, a sexual fantasy, much like a dream, is relatively uncontrollable, as each time you try to visualize it, it changes itself and has to be brought back to fit in with your deep desire.

But a memory is something that you can stop dreaming about, stop remembering about, rewind, go back to the beginning, or fast forward to the very end, and do this time and time again, year in, year out; yet it always stays the very same, day in, day out, year in, year out. And now for fifty odd years, my memories of past lives have always stayed the same! If I now rewind my memories to my primary school years I can remember my first friend, John Caddock, and my second best friend, Andrew Coleman, and my first girlfriend, Elizabeth Chapel. If I rewind some more I can remember lying in my cot as a baby and colours, like wet paint, rushing in under the bedroom door and spreading out over the bedroom walls and over the curtains; and before that I tried to stand up, but was extremely disappointed to have legs of marshmallows. Rewind my mind further back and I remember standing in front of a book which had information about different lives and physical attributes revealing themselves in long lines across the pages; in other words, I remember receiving strands of genetic material, my DNA—one very odd thing here which should reverberate around the world for a bit within the scientific community. I believe that I could even choose from different strands of deoxyribonucleic acid. Choose physical strength over intelligence, choose to be Male or Female, and choose items of character right at the moment of conception!

I first started trying to work it out in my teenage years, treating it all like a jigsaw puzzle that you can piece together, but back then absolutely no-one was the slightest bit interested. Then I started toying with the story again in **1993**, (when I was thirty two), on my very first word processor—a story I wrote very badly but nevertheless produced the first draft edition, spiral bound, and then self-published the first thirty pages of my memories of past lives in 1997 which I called... *Manmade God* (ISBN 0953055701).

When you are trying to give some evidence to prove some supernatural phenomena, it is very important that some paper evidence exists to support the claims you are making. That is exactly how I see my first publication of **Manmade God ISBN 0953055701.** Copies exist in the National Library of Scotland, the National Library of Wales, the Bodleian Library in Oxford, the Trinity College Library, Dublin, and the Cambridge University Library, West Road, Cambridge CB39 DR. (Legal Deposit Receipts still intact & in order.)

However, it has not been until now that I believe that I can truly write about what I remember and about what seems to have happened to me. Now that I have lots of support and encouragement from my close friends and my own family, I intend to do this amazing phenomenon some justice. I do now think that I can understand just how it does happen and what amazing force powers it. It's not easy just to blurt it out to the Western World; it has to be expressed, rather precisely and most exactly right. So, I found that I needed to write about it again to achieve some real clarity on the matter and give it some proper structure; in one sense I needed to see it on paper myself.

...So, out of some devilment or out of my own embarrassment, whichever it was, I attributed my own previous life memories to my fictional character Peter Miller.

The years really do pass by quickly. I am going to be fifty-two years old this year, and I feel that it is definitely the right time to confess the whole amazing truth about the odd things in my mind before anything unsavoury happens to me. I must say that I tried hard to have a normal life—I so wanted acceptance and praise from my parents. So I was perhaps too embarrassed about it to write down all the gory details before this time in my own name—not wanting to be criticised over it again, or accused of being a complete fool by the **philistines** of this world. If I was born and bred in India, then it would not have been so hard to talk about, as all traditional Indian beliefs include a continuous cycle of life and death!

...However, I did write about it. In the end I could not stop myself from thinking about it, or from trying to understand how the spirit world works. I needed to learn how to explain what I feel inside and if you believe that you can even remember being conceived—yes, that very moment when a singular spermatozoa successfully breaks through the egg wall and delivers the strings of DNA. Things do become very hard to explain for a builder, so I gave my own memories to my character Peter Miller and again published the details of my mind's own experience of previous lives in February of 2012 in *The Three Lives of Peter Miller.*

But here and now it seems to be the right time to tell my story straight; it is my intention to try and explain just how the spirit world works, how it is possible to remember previous lives, explain how one can travel through the underworld and have **out-of-the-body experiences!**

It is a fact that these memories of previous lives have always been with me, ever since my birth here into this life; they have always been in full colour with all the sounds and smells of the events encountered and complete with the remembered inner loneliness, turmoil, fear and the other complex emotions felt at the time of the events.

I remember being (outwardly anyway), other people at different times through history and in different places. Internally though, it was always *me*, myself; it is like a continuous flow of one's own conscious experience— memories, including working on and falling off, by accident, from the rigging of a tall ship and drowning in the very cold seawater and then in another lifetime it was mostly about the war and of slaughter and millions of pointless deaths, of being trapped in the trenches.

Memories of crawling through narrow trenches lugging my rifle along through the mud, digging tunnels, cleaning my muddy boots and fighting against the enemy hoards, field guns and tanks and the painful memory of dying next to the front-line trenches of World War One.

And if that revelation was not enough to engage your interest, and I know it will sound like a completely crazy tale, I also seem to remember lying on the wet grass, dying—and whilst being dead, for a very long time, before I was actually born into this life, at my birth, actually forty-three years (or say fifty years) too late to have such memories of the First World War.

So what exactly is the Human Mind? Unique in all of this

18

world, yes, perhaps unique in the entire universe? But how does it really *work*, how does it manifest this constant churning thought process? What is the mind made of and *where* exactly is it?

I doubt that you ever really forget anything and I am wondering where are all of your memories are kept? Are your memories likely to be kept in DNA or in the Electrical properties of your mind?

If I actually can remember being conceived, then the mind and your memory must exist without any physical brain matter; and that is exactly what I am telling you! But all these questions are difficult for anyone to answer. My memories of the First World War (in Chapter Eight), my memories of being conceived in the womb (Chapters 10 and 12) are there as evidence of this continuous consciousness of the life essence.

I am asking if your individual thinking and emotional mind— your individual thinking and reasoning memory-making, opinion-making individual personality—constitutes what the Bible refers to as the Soul. I know that some believe our thinking minds are the inner self, a minuscule fragment of the **Holy Ghost!**

Through these years of trying to understand my own inner feelings, control my own emotions and analyse these strange memories in my own head that I know are not of my own manufacture and perhaps should not really be in there, whilst trying to find a true meaning to my life, along with some additional reading and research into our history, our philosophy and discovering the world of psychology, I have come to a stage whereby I can 'at least' attempt to explain what I have come to believe to be true.

The Human Mind appears to be one part physical and one part spiritual, both natural and supernatural working together in a life, combined... I do not believe that my memories of former lives are in any way delusional, because I have always remembered them, since before being of school age and if I give any evidence at all, then it all comes from long before I was ever aware of what spirituality meant, or before knowing what Heaven or Hell was meant to be.

On my travels I have discovered mythology (collections of detailed beliefs in things supernatural and to us improbable) and many of the world mythologies tell tales of immortality and spiritual journeys through the underworld. Also, I have noted that many of the world's oldest religions include the belief that the mind/soul does live on—in some form or another after the death of the body. This notion has existed since the time of the powerful Pharaohs of the first Egyptian Dynasties, whose entire civilization was built on the understanding that our spiritual existence on this earth is ephemeral (transitory). The work of secret societies in this day and age is not so secret, and various religious sects the world over have persistently believed in the immortality of the spirit within. And if my discoveries are true, then the mind/soul may have no real or solid attachment to the brain or to the earth-bound body, but may be a completely separate entity altogether.

Out of the body experiences have been openly written about and published by people from all walks of life and from all nations of the world. It apparently happens whilst meditating or after an accident or during a complicated surgical procedure. Some people, many people in fact, also freely admit to remembering details of previous lives and more surprisingly, nearly everyone **under hypnosis** remembers past lives, often in great detail. You may instantly revolt against this idea and revel in your own negativity, but perhaps for your own benefit you should not revolt against it but consider it objectively instead. Perhaps all is not lost in the mists of time as I really do believe there are many subtle indicators pointing us towards the truth about our spirituality!

In his early writings, **Homer** referred to the immortal soul. (See *Human Immortality and the Redemption of Death* by Simon Tugwell.)

Everybody has the ability to feel happy or sad, to think, reason, calculate, desire, imagine, daydream, lie, deceive, remember whole hoards of things and fantasize about different lifestyles and erotic liaisons and have self-awareness, because everybody has a mind capable of doing such amazing things. Yet, every single movement, every single thought and every single mental function depends directly on your ability to remember. Your mind could not perform a single function if you instantly forget what you are doing and that which you have already done.

Most of that which your mind does is in the subconscious: you never know how much goes on down there, controlling necessary bodily functions, keeping us alive and at times influencing or mating habits! Our minds also give us complex positive emotions like, love, desire, devotion, lust, kindness, generosity, as well as negative emotions like envy, jealousy, embarrassment, as easily as hate, revenge, self-loathing; and sometimes our minds also lead us to suicide and murder.

On a lighter note, some people in conversation suggest that they may have spirit guides and often feel like they are being watched. Some people believe they can see into the future, predict the future, whilst others (mediums) believe they can even communicate with the souls of the dead!

Perhaps we should all be inclined to examine our memories, our inner feelings, our spiritual selves by talking about out-of-body experiences, and the odd, perhaps out-of-character memories of former lives and distant lands, and call in the aid of modern science to realise fundamental earthly powers which universally unite everything on this Earth and in the Heavens. I am assuming that most level-headed people will say 'there are no magical or invisible timeless energies on the earth because they cannot be seen.'

Well, strangely, most of us are oblivious to the fact that the earth is (by its very nature) an enormous electric dynamo spinning at great speed in space causing electro-magnetic energy to be generated by the movement of molten iron in the Earth's outer core and which also produces energy and releases radiation which in turn generates a magnetic field on the surface. (Google search: geodynamo and our magnetosphere.) The effect is to constantly be charging and discharging currents between the Earth's surface and our atmosphere.

Electric currents induced in the ionosphere also generate magnetic fields. (Google search: ionospheric dynamo region.)

One very positive effect of this electrical generation is the geomagnetic field which surrounds the Earth (the magnetosphere) and protects us from solar flares, cosmic rays and ultraviolet radiation that could very badly damage our atmosphere, our climate and our environment. (More about that perhaps in a later chapter.)

So, on the Earth's surface and around the Earth's crust, we have our own electromagnetic field in which we live. (Magnetic fields appear over anything that has an electric charge.) This electromagnetic field flows through the earth and around the earth and constantly flows through everything, through the oceans, through the land, through everything living and even through us and always has done, 24/7.

So it is a proven fact that there is an invisible, yet omnipresent, ubiquitous, powerful force on the Earth that we cannot see, hear or feel, yet it is with us and inside of us! Everything has energy within its basic components, either trapped or flowing, through buildings, houses, churches, bridges, and roads, tunnels and mine shafts and underground caverns, along with trees, flowers, streams, rivers, lakes and even larger bodies of water, and each of these things has energy which in turn creates its own surrounding magnetic field.

In other words, our whole world probably has another dimension to it, which is formed of just the structure of the pure energy within it, but, its form is exactly the same shape as our world.

All I am suggesting is that mythological tales of the underworld, the next world, the afterlife and the spiritual world all make reference to something that does actually exist but perhaps you have to be dead to see...

It is not so obvious to everyone that within our mortal/physical bodies we must use at least a tiny proportion of this ever-flowing electrical charge within our muscles and our minds as the auto-motive force that stimulates our own movements, our growth and our own thoughts and more to the point, it is that all-important spark of life in a new-born child!

I am no scientist, I am not a scholar, not even an academic person; at the very best I perhaps have an over-developed sense of self-awareness and a great sense of personal identity; however, it seems very reasonable for me to think that your mind, your psyche, your spiritual being, is powered by a tiny amount of this energy which you should regard as your own soul.

All I am attempting to do here, is to observe the human condition, make a personal study of my own motivation, self-analyse my own perspective of this world, tell the truth about some of my own memories and mental experiences, and try to explain just how it could possibly be true and even beneficial to believe.

The smallest brain with the slightest interest in world religions and/or mythology of the ancient world would readily recognise strikingly similar ideas and beliefs held by all, which point to an ever-present but invisible force, a timeless spiritual form, a powerful force more than capable of carrying you from this life through the underworld and on into the next world!

Many years ago the invisible world which surrounds us must have seemed very much closer to the individual than it does to us today. We, here in this life have been swallowed up in a world of industry—technology, progress, materialism and self-importance. But back in the days of the hunter and the gatherer, the gardener and the farmer, when the ringing of church bells were the loudest manmade sound ever to be heard in the land, any peasant worker, landowner and traveller alike would have been very much more aware of the magic in the earth beneath their feet.

Spirits of the earth and sky all would have hovered on the verge of being wicked, spirits of the dead would have lived in the hedgerows, in the dark woods and in deserted cottages and everybody would have accepted it as natural.

In every part of the world the spiritual remains of the dead would have been presumed to live somewhere, perhaps in a slightly different dimension but with us still, beneath our feet in sacred burial grounds, trapped in the fires of Hell or residing at the side of God in Heaven. Throughout all of history no people ever accepted that mortal death was the actual end of a person's life, but was regarded as the beginning of a new chapter or journey.

Witches and Warlocks of the past, and Spiritual Priests and Scientist Priests could summon these spirits to appear, or advise humans on the correct religious practise to conciliate them.

The underworld, as written about by the **Minoans**, the **Egyptians** and the **Ancient Greeks,** to our understanding is the dreaded region ruled over by Hades, wearer of the Helmet of Darkness and owner of all the buried wealth underground. Hermes, the messenger of the gods and the God of Cunning, luck and theft, escorts the spirits of the dead to the Underworld.

They enter it by crossing the River Acheron, but if their relations have not given them a coin to pay the ferryman they must wander forever on the gloomy shores.

Several ordeals await them as they grope their way through the dark caverns beyond the river. They must drink from the River Lethe, whose waters make them forget their previous lives on earth, and then face the three-headed dog Cerberus whose mouth dribbles black venom. If they do not have cakes of Barley and Honey to feed him they will spend eternity at his mercy.

Then the spirits have to pass by the three terrible judges of the dead, who decide their eternal fates. Those who have committed unnatural crimes will be tormented forever by the winged daughters of the Night whose hair is a mass of hissing serpents.

The other sinners are thrown into the rivers of woe, wailing and flames. The ghosts of those who were neither good nor bad are sent to wander eternity on the bleak plains where the only flowers are the black lilies of asphodel.

...The only spirits released by Hades are those of very virtuous men and women who go on to the Elysian Fields and there spend eternity in a perpetual joyous summer.

Today we have a theory that myths and legends were invented

on purpose only to explain natural phenomena that exist but may still be hard to see, describe or understand. The seriousness of this belief is demonstrated by the huge amount of information available of other worlds and of the other beings that co-exist with us on the Earth both above the ground and beneath it

Is it possible that these ancient myths about spiritual journeys to the next world and legends of mystical journeys by boat along underground rivers and adventures fighting demons lurking in the underworld, were invented just to explain (through-all-time) the normal natural events by which we can travel through the world without any material or physical form and find our way back to the surface of the earth and to be born again to a new life...

The Ancient Philosopher **Plato** himself made many references to the Immortal soul....

CHAPTER THREE

Have you ever had an Out-of-Body Experience? The big question for mankind is, of course, can we really be immortal? Can the soul of a man really survive bodily death just like the Ancient Scientist Priests of the mystery schools of Greece and of Ancient Egypt taught to their young initiates? (Initiates often being the offspring of the Nobles and high ranking civil servants.) The physical biological body will always burn out eventually, even in the future when failing body parts are even easier to replace. But can your soul really reincarnate as somebody new straight after mortal death, or does it have to take many years? Is it possible that this invisible inner spiritual energy that we use in life to animate a flesh and blood physical being through a lifetime of experience, is naturally recycled at a later date, and may unwittingly be used by some other unrelated creature, mammal, bird, or other living thing to animate its physical body?

Because I can remember my former lives, it is very obvious to me that the answer is one or the other of these two questions. It is either by choice, or by accident, but either way, it does happen. I can easily say this, because I have some evidence within myself that the spiritual world does exist, and that it flows through the earth as naturally as water flows downhill and that we humans most probably have an immortal soul that can be continuously aware of itself and of its environment.

Starting with my choice of cover picture of this book; this picture intentionally depicts a young but very dead Prussian Soldier; back then he would have been part of the German Central Forces (in the early19th century, Prussia emerged as the most powerful German state) of the First World War. At that time it had been overcast and raining almost continually for many weeks, so the body of this young man is lying in very wet grass, somewhere between a coppice of thin trees and the edge of the muddy front line trenches in or around the time of May-June-1917.

The poor boy had an errand to run for the commandant's pleasure, and in a moment of quiet he slipped unnoticed up and out of the muddy trenches and away under the shadow of a coppice of thin trees where he felt momentarily euphoric (momentarily extremely jubilant or happy); but then a shot rang out and he lost his life as a consequence of his actions and he lay there contemplating death all alone in the wet grass.

However, this picture is not just a convenient image of a dead soldier at a time and a place in our history to facilitate a young man's tale of woe, not in the least. This picture is in fact one tiny fraction of a mass of memories from that time that I have in my mind now, and have carried around in my mind for all of my life.

...I will say again, and perhaps to coin a phrase, **a dream is something you might try to hang onto, yet it will always**

slip away from you time after time: a memory is something that you can stop, rewind, or fast forward, yet it always remains the same. This is because you know every second of it and you are aware of every tiny detail of it!

As honestly as I can explain it, I believe that I know that man's life intimately; I remember his thoughts, his feelings and his own intimate mannerisms (which are exactly like mine). I know of his homeland, his brothers and sisters, and I remember his mother baking homemade bread and that delicious smell from the brick oven.

He was about seventeen years old when he died, a friendly if slightly foolish lad. He died around the time of April/May 1917, so he was born right at the turn of the nineteenth century. I really do believe that this young but dead soldier was me, or is still a part of me now, because I have within me the memories of all of his life and the memories of the very end of *his* previous life—or is that the end of *my* previous life?

My memories of this lad's life and death become more and more peculiar as that poor young soldier lay there dead in the grass as the war waged on all around him. However, he lay there dead but he could not completely pass over, and continued strangely conscious and he never ever lost that inner consciousness...

Dying or dead, his **mind** continued with what is now called its **conscious narrative,** of the events unfolding around him, even though his mortal body never moved itself again.

In his mind he knew he was so badly wounded that his body could not survive, and consequently, just lay there waiting for his spirit to pass away; but his spirit did not pass over.

I know that in this boy's mind he could still hear the guns of the war, the Howitzers, the rumble of the tank tracks and the men shouting for many more weeks, if not for many more months afterwards. Eventually, all did grow peaceful and still; that was when all around the battlefield and all the Earth seemed to be covered and surrounded with a white velvet mist, like that of a fresh dewy spring morning!

In this life you can drive your car too fast and pick up a fine and points on your licence for doing so; you can argue with your girlfriend or with your wife and get a conviction for battery or an assault. You might find yourself with no trade and unemployed, living on state benefits, and you can try to steal something from another and you can be sent to prison for your crimes—and that is all considered to be very normal; but the one big thing that you must never do is say 'out loud with any amount of conviction' that you have already lived a life and died before!

Obviously, as a child in this country, recounting a tale of being part of the Central Forces in World War One did not impress my peers. However, it seems that many people have, or as I now understand, do have memories of previous lives, which are generally revealed under hypnosis.

However, apparently that is still not regarded as enough evidence to prove the existence of a previous life or previous lives. Yet, I have never been to a hypnotist and never have been hypnotised. I prefer not to let other people delve into my mind for fear of having any part of my personality altered or my memories damaged.

Still, I have easily remembered my life as a young soldier in the First World War, boarding a black train for the journey from my homeland to the front line, creeping and crawling through the dark and through all the mud with my rifle in hand—ever since being a very small child.

Another question then: being really honest, do you have or have you ever thought that you have memories inside of your head that you know for certain really ought to belong to someone else? If you have had odd memories, have you discounted them as delusion, dreams or mere fantasy?

Do you by chance remember having different parents, different brothers and sisters, a different childhood experience altogether! Do you remember climbing into a Black Railway cattle truck with many other soldiers to start on the long journey to the fight on the front line combined with a terrible dread felt deep within? Do you remember the horses pulling the carts full of ammunition being stuck in the mud? Do you remember the terrible roaring thunder of Metal Battle Tanks, racing past you heading towards the enemy on the Front Line? Do you remember the fear? The smell? The desperation? The pointlessness? The Duty to your Country? No? Well, I do remember these things and so much more besides.

I remember being shot in my left side from behind and falling down onto the long grass and slowly dying in unimaginable agony whilst the war around me waged on, and I could only mentally question God's existence and ponder upon the reasons that men go to war with each other and why our universe even exists!

Of course, it could all be mere fantasy or a complex mental delusion brought about by some trauma at birth, but I seriously doubt it; if I am discovered to be mad, then fine, but, what if I am right about this? The reality is that many lives could be made over again and many people might not be so afraid of death!

I have been analysing myself for many years, yet have found nothing to account for these memories, no head trauma from any accident and there was no brainwashing by any other 'believers'; my family was never religious and there was never any mention of God or of the Holy Ghost in our house, so this is not any sort of induced fantasy, surely?... So what if this is real? If it is as real as I believe, then it is evidence that the world population should take into account a spiritual continuity after death, and that is a really important statement.

Continuing through my memories of that time, I also remember lying there in the grass for such a very long time, weeks, months, years, I could not possibly say. However, I was still lying there after the war was over, and I remember thinking that I could actually hear the grass and weeds growing right through my rotting corpse, with the wind also whistling through my mind. Don't think for a moment that I am over-dramatizing this event; that is exactly as I recall it and it was, so I believe, one of the reasons why I remember it so clearly.... It was the very sound of the grass growing through me and the wind whistling through my mind which ultimately kept me— my mind or my spiritual soul—conscious, thinking, active and awake. Is it just by coincidence, that now, many, many years later, scientists believe that our universe makes some kind of background noise—white noise?

So as best I can work it out, it was the sounds of the earth itself which then had irritated me, and kept my spirit awake **(or stopped me from falling into an ignorant eternal sleep)** and proves, to me anyway, that the soul can or does survive death.

But again there is much more to it than that, in the belief that I do not think that whilst I was dead, that I ever lost my self-awareness! Not from the moment of being shot in 1917 to this very moment today, which is ninety-six years later!

The writings of **Euripides** contain many references to the immortal soul...

There are of course several different ways of looking at reincarnation; there is the natural way, the unnatural way and the spiritual way!

The first way is to believe the Buddhists' romantic notion of the immortal soul that continually seeks life, interaction, connection and purpose until you follow on the path of enlightenment. Or another way of looking at this, is to think of the mind and inner workings of the spirit as being internally powered by a timeless force that manifests itself as continuous self-awareness of its journey through the universe.

...Or in the third way, as was the understanding of the Athenians, that the inner spirit not only has its own identity, but is also influenced by its first religious beliefs possibly dating back thousands of years and that the gods of our past really can give you new life and also to set your soul tasks to triumph over.

The memories I have are very real memories of former lives, but I am not sure if it could be put down to the recycling of energy that my mind is using, giving me the impression of previous lives...Which would be a terrible shame as I prefer to believe in the gods of the Athenians.

I swear on my life that this is not a fictional tale. Why would I go to so much trouble to explain my embarrassment at the thought of being labelled insane, delusional, stupid or even far too romantic for a construction worker, and anyway, from where did I get it all from if it is not true?

And if it is all true, and all human-beings have a continuous awareness of experience, then why isn't everybody else writing about their continuous experiences and about memories of past lives?

The imagination is a wonderful thing; we all have imagination but that is the point—to imagine some other event or other location, you are only speculating without inside knowledge, whereas I remember living the life in a German state, in an industrial town where all the walls and all of the windows of the houses were covered in thick black soot from our industry.

I remember being the oldest of the children, the terraced house where we lived, the desolate front garden and the well-stocked back garden full of vegetable and salad crops and memories of throwing stones and breaking windows, the cobbled streets and the baker's shop.

All this and much more besides, I am not imagining things that I do not know. I am actually remembering what I have seen, what I have heard and that which I have experienced…

But then on the other hand, maybe I have somehow been given a head start in the search for the truth about our continual awareness of existence and our true spirituality? Because as well as believing that I have lived before, in this life I also **had an accident** here, which led to an out of the body experience, which for me proved beyond a doubt that your thinking-feeling-personal-spiritual form can exist outside of the mortal body.

During an out-of-body-experience, everything that you feel you are within, at least, temporarily exists outside of your physical body, leaving your mind to consider its position, which it seems cannot stray too far from the injured and unconscious body.

Obviously after many years of contemplation I am now a firm believer in the continual existence of the soul as a separate entity from the body. I believe that it is true and that it is a natural process that the human spirit or the soul, (if you prefer to call it that) can live on indefinitely with or without physical form, but the problem, as always has been, is proving this as a fact.

They will say that nobody has come back; but I have come back.

Here in this book I am coming out of the closet, no matter how many people are going to find my words laughable or say that I am just misinformed. I have come back and my story cannot be kept secret indefinitely; it has to be told, and I am going to be very honest in telling you what I know and try to explain it as best that I can, give you all the facts and you can then decide for yourself.

However, this is not just my story; my account of previous lives can only add a little more weight to the philosophical arguments about what spirituality is, and what the immortal soul might actually be. My story is also about messages hidden in mythology and information concealed in some of the oldest belief systems of the Human Race from millennia ago, and I have also incorporated some fascinating aspects of the workings of the human mind from my own first-hand experience...

For most of us this is a very confusing place. There are just too many negative experiences to suffer from, even in the very first years of life, too many accidents waiting to happen, too many problems to face up to and so much negative and wrong information that we are forced to take on board. We are regimentally taught exactly what we should believe in, how we should behave, and how well you should perform, that these days young people rarely know who they are or what they want to achieve from just one lifetime.

It seems that **our reality** is often exactly what other people say that it is; in fact, this reality we are told to believe in, is such a negative experience for most of us, that if you had a previous life, and if you were born with some unique memories of the spirit world, then all that you once were, all that you should have remembered and all the presence of mind that you started life with, is very likely to be completely driven out of you..

As in my case: for so many years I was too busy conforming to other people's expectations of me to admit a different perspective of life or to communicate my belief in the afterlife. The real world then becomes shrouded from view and mystical systems which allow us to exist in the first place are long forgotten!

As a child you assume that your parents and the adults amongst us belong to the right religion, know exactly what they are talking about, and that they care about their own offspring with a passion. But then, when you grow up you realise that they don't, and that there are very few facts about our life on this earth that everybody agrees with anyway. Scientist disagree with Philosophers, Doctors often disagree with Psychologists, Astrologists disagree with Idealists, Methodist disagree with Puritans and the Politicians disagree with trade unionists, and religion is always at odds with science when it should not be. I am convinced that there was a time when science and religion was one and the same thing. My only wish now is to try to bring science and religion back together again!

However, it happens to be a fact that if you are looking for gold in this world you do have to dig a really deep hole in the ground and move lots of unwanted rubbish out of the way before you really find anything truly valuable. Finding the truth about something is just as difficult as finding *gold* in the ground as there is plenty of unwanted rubbish to move away. The rubbish is all of the religious dogma, the religious doctrine and the pompousness brought about by our Tudor our Victorian eras.

In my own opinion, to ever stand any chance of discovering the truth about your own spiritual form you first have to forget all that you have been told to believe in and start again by analysing that which you know only you could have brought to this wonderful place...

Forget that you are a mortal, forget that you are fragile and start thinking about being a descendant of the Great Egyptian Empire or one of the Athenians or even that you are descendant of the American Indians... Search your mind for that little bit of memory that only you could have brought along from another life. The smallest fragment of a memory or a distant place is enough to re-start your own self-belief; you must be positive, believe in it and nurture it like you would an acorn which you want to grow into a **mighty Oak.**

For some reason I have always thought that mankind's pre-history has been deliberately and completely muddled up. It's all confused now and the real knowledge—the real truth about our origin, our abilities, our spirituality and perhaps even the knowledge of our destiny as a race—has been not only buried in time but lost forever. It seems to me that the people of the

Ancient World knew it was true. The Egyptians, the Sumerian, the Aztecs and the Greeks all knew the truth about mystical forces, all carved fine statues of men and gods with wings, yet today that knowledge is gone.

Somehow the world has become divided into the physical world and the spiritual world, with the belief in dualism. By my very nature, I believe that this world, although made up of two different things, should be understood as one and the same thing; our world is a unity, and we are all a combination of the solid and the invisible.

We are altogether really amazing (for me); we are a combination of the natural flesh and the eternal supernatural spirit.

I also believe that I have been given a special task by my gods and if I have not been given a task to perform by the gods, then why is it still hardwired into my very biology, into my very personality and into my own life ambitions…

To elucidate further, I have always wanted to find some way to explain how your mind, how your individual identity and your spiritual personality really works, even when it is outside of the body. Trust me when I say that it is easier for me to believe in this than it is for me to explain it, but I must try.

From my own **out-of-body** experience, I can say to you with lots of confidence that everything that you think you are (your mind, memory, soul, spirit and personality), all that is not solid or part of your physical form, can and will still exist without the physical body.

You can think, remember, worry, feel your own emotions, be self-aware, communicate with other spirits and even have a panic attacks whilst outside of the body. How you think, your self-awareness, your own self-image, your emotional states, your memories and your unique personality, your feelings for others, are all your own and they all stay together (connected and unique) and functioning even out of the body!

I can say this because my body was lifeless, lying there flat on the road, and to this day I believe that my conscious personality was up on the roof of the building from which I had fallen. **Actually hanging onto the roof tiles** and the guttering with my imaginary hands and arms would be a much more accurate description of what was happening to me, yet I was still aware of the events which had caused my accident, and also within me there was much concern for my own future before being instantly returned into my mortal flesh. I can only hazard a guess that I hit my head on the surface of the road and was rendered temporarily unconscious. The unexpected but consequential jolt allowed my soul to 'bump out' rather than 'jump out' of my body and floated rather quickly up into the air, around four stories up (perhaps twelve meters).

As I said, I was very much aware of the accident. I was very aware of the separation of my mind from my physical body, and aware of my physical body elsewhere, somewhere indirectly beneath me being in some difficulty (possibly dying or dead) which led me, my still conscious mind that is, to seriously worry about my future life. Worry rapidly grew into panic, and I was aware of being very concerned about my immediate future, of the prospect of being spiritual with no home or no specific place to be, and consequently considering ways whereby I might be able to get back to my body. I remember thinking about my virtually invisible spiritual limbs in relation to my immediate need to hang on to the roof tiles and I remember believing that I actually still had the use of my hands and my arms. I am quite sure now that it was just habit formed over years of physical activity. Obviously the spiritual form within is made of that other thing, anti-matter or Holy Spirit and has no particular size or shape; it's probably just the energy or life force that you have been using to operate the body, temporarily outside of the body.

I wrote about my **out-of-body experience** in *The Three Lives of Peter Miller*... The time and location are different to my own experience; however, the actual inner thoughts and feelings, whilst out of the body, are the very same. I will reveal the exact date and details of my own experience in a later chapter.

For now, though, I just want to introduce you to Peter Miller's story... (from Chapter Three, pages 56-7). **I quote:**

> I had a load of about six tons of wheat on-board the trailer and this one time when I was unloading the wheat into a drying bin using a three-phase electric auger, I was electrocuted! You had to tip the trailer up by hydraulic pressure from the tractor and I started emptying the grain into a small square steel bin. Then I started the motor of the auger by pushing a lever down onto a mark called 'first phase', then after a few moments pulled the same lever up to a mark called 'second phase' before finally pushing it all the way up to the 'run' position.

It's all very well and good most times, but on this particular day I pushed the lever up from 'second phase' to its run position when an electric shock ripped through my hand and up my arm taking my breath away, shooting me back about five feet leaving me unconscious, I think!

For some very strange reason I could see my body laid out 'seemingly dead' beneath me, legs and arms motionless, my eyes shut, my hair being blown around by the breeze. I was, or rather my conscious mind, was now some thirty feet above my body, and hanging onto the edge of the asbestos roof covering the grain store.

I was still thinking, reasoning and had a great concern for my mortal body, thinking that there were no people about to help, resuscitate my body or to call for an ambulance. My conscious thinking soul was out of my body, thrown out by the jolt of electricity and now up in the air...

The wind and the dust swirled through my thoughts as it had once before, after I had died on the battlefield in France.

An extract from my second book – The 3 Lives of Peter Miller.

It will sound very much like a cliché, but it does seem to me that the inner spiritual self, really can **jump out of your skin, and not just survive, reason and think, but also be able**

to observe the new situation and make and store new memories of this supernatural event!

It strikes me to wonder, when the spirit is outside of the physical body, where these new memories are stored, when you are detached from your mortal frame and normal brain function. Luckily I was returned into my flesh and blood body when it was resuscitated by an ambulance man (this was in the summer of 1987 on the corner of Manor Road and Mount Pleasant Road).

I was taken by ambulance to the Royal East-Sussex Hospital where I discharged myself after several hours and took a Taxi home where I spent the next two weeks in bed!

Supernatural has connotations of Ghostlike—Phantasmal—Spiritual, and anything that science today cannot yet understand; however, all other civilizations from our ancient history have believed in spiritual forms and the Supernatural...

The Cambridge Encyclopaedia explains that the Supernatural or Paranormal is beyond the bounds of what can be explained in terms of currently-held scientific knowledge.

Thus to describe an event as paranormal or supernatural requires that all other possible explanations for the event, based on known principles of science, be completely ruled out. However, the term does not imply that an eventual explanation will not ever be found as science discovers more about allegedly paranormal events year on year.

All people have an individual character and a unique personality; we call this an indication of being human, but what if it's not that simple! What if it is an indication—symptom, if you like—of having a spirit inside of you that is unique, immortal and still growing, learning and developing? What would be cruel is if you did die and you were gone forever.

No, I cannot accept that. We are unique and we have to have timeless spiritual forms. One day you learn through schooling, religion or from films that the Devil, Lucifer, Satan has a number **666.** If that is fantasy or fiction, it does not matter; but if there is any truth in this number, then we all have a number of creation...

In other words, when the Devil came into being, 665 other people had already been born into this world. So we can just ignore this or question it; if you question it, then we all might have a number.

The thing is, if you have an immortal soul that continues on indefinitely through time, how was it created? And if it turns out that we each have been created by someone or something, might we not have our own exact number of creation, a number that identifies us for-all-time, should we ever find our way to judgement day in front of God!

Moving on just for the moment: we have so many thoughts, feelings, emotions, memories, calculations, opinions and expectations produced from just a few moments of brain activity—it is amazing. Your mind continually produces a story-like narrative which is the ultimate expression of that which you are experiencing as life. Your mind is astronomically, mathematically and systematically amazing, and that's long before you ever learn how to paint a masterpiece on canvas, start writing poetry or your prize-winning book.

Our minds are forward thinking, problem solving, manipulating, selfish, probability computers that use memories of previous events and emotions felt, to calculate the probable outcome of new opportunities, to discover and plan new ventures.

We gauge all that we know upon the basis of things that we have heard, seen, read or felt emotionally; we rely upon our memories of experience, or memories of learnt facts, but then in the night we wake up in a terrible sweat, frightened out of our skin! Why? Because we have been imagining—or dreaming—that there are snakes, worms and beetles in our bed and each crawling or wriggling all over our bodies! But then, why is this? Is it imagination of the worst kind, or is it still memories being randomly selected by your subconscious mind?

Then again, I remember being shot dead and left by the trenches of the First World War! The point is, could I really still have been consciously aware of my surroundings when my body was just a limp, lifeless corpse? But I remember a sort of semi-conscious awareness all of the time, allowing me to make memories of worms, snakes and beetles all creeping and crawling through my rotting carcase.

I am, of course, suggesting that our conscious thinking, reasoning, remembering mind may still be active and aware of its surroundings for a long period of time after death.

I swear on my natural normal life that I have had perfectly clear memories inside of my head of being another person, living a very natural and normal life in another land, of growing up being a member of another family, and of signing up for service and fighting along the front line during the First World War since the very day that I was born. How could this be possible?

The Spirit continues to live on after death.

CHAPTER FOUR

Spirits, Spiritual faith, Spiritual People, Spiritualism and Spiritualists!... Here, before moving on, I need to make some comparisons between Spiritual people and what is called Spiritualism as a world faith. As I understanding things, the term, Spiritual people, refers to people like myself, who believe that the soul survives mortal death of the body, leaving the soul free to progress on its journey through time and space, as itself or in reincarnation within a new body. Whereas Spiritualism as a world faith generally refers to people who believe that some people can communicate with the spirits of the dead!

I would not be able to contain my beliefs to just one of these two different trains of thought, as I too believe that, for a short period after death at the very least, that Shamans and Mediums with a special gift can communicate with the spirits of the recently departed and the very recently dead.

...So, when I write that I am a 'spiritual person', or that I am a spiritualist, I am not suggesting that I am a medium and can speak to the spirits of the dead; instead, I am only saying that I do believe that the soul can live on after the mortal death of the host body and that I believe the soul of a man has a continuing existence of self-awareness.

As far as I know, I have only once spoken with the spirit of a dead person, and that was on the other side after I myself had been shot and killed in the war and had myself passed over into the spirit world.

★ ★ ★

The Mind and the Memory: So what, then, exactly is the mind, and how is it related to the physical body?

From *The Undiscovered Mind* by John Horgan:
The mind (also referred to as the soul or the psyche) was originally supposed to differentiate between animate and inanimate nature; **Aristotle** (Greek philosopher, scientist and physician c.448-c.388 BC) thought that plants and animals also had souls. However, much later philosophers ascribed the mind only to humans, proposing that it was the one thing that unifies our experiences, makes our experiences ours (and not some other persons), makes self-consciousness and self-awareness possible, initiates our actions and defines us as human beings.... [p. 795] *Cambridge Encyclopaedia*.

So, how is it composed?

Reading from *Structure of the Mind* by Sigmund Freud; from the book *Abnormal Psychology*, by Gerald C, Davidson & John M. Neale. Page 30:

Sigmund Freud divided the mind, or the psyche, into

three principal parts, **id, ego,** and **superego.** These are figures of speech (metaphors) for specific functions or energies! According to Sigmund Freud, the **id** is present at birth and is the part of the mind that accounts for all the energy needed to run the psyche. It comprises of the basic urges for food, water, elimination, warmth, affection, and sex. Trained as a neurologist, Freud saw the source of all of id's energy as biological. Only later, as the infant develops, is the energy, which he called libido, converted into psychic energy, all of it unconscious, below the level of awareness. The id seeks immediate gratification, operating on what Freud called the pleasure principle. When the id is not satisfied tension is produced, and the id strives to eliminate this tension as quickly as possible.

The next aspect of the psyche that develops is the **ego.** Unlike the id, the ego is primarily conscious and begins to develop from the id during the second six months of life. Whereas the id resorts to fantasy if necessary, the task of the ego is to deal with reality. The ego does not employ primary process thinking, for fantasy will not keep the organism alive. Through its planning and decision-making functions, called secondary process thinking, the ego realizes that operating the pleasure principle at all times, as the id would like to do, is not the most effective way of maintaining life. The ego thus operates on the reality principle as it mediates between the demands of reality and the immediate gratification desired by the **id.**

The final part of the psyche that emerges is the **super-ego,** which operates roughly as our conscience and develops throughout childhood. Freud believed that the superego developed from the ego, much as the ego develops out of the id. As children discover that many of their impulses, such as biting and bed-wetting, are not acceptable to their parents, they begin to take on, or introject parental values as their own, in order to enjoy parental approval and to avoid disapproval.

The behaviour of the human being, as conceptualized by Freud, is thus a complex interplay of three parts of the psyche, all vying for achievement of goals that cannot always be reconciled. The interplay of these forces is referred to as the **psychodynamics** of the personality. Theorists who follow some of Freud's ideas are also referred to as psychodynamic theorists. Freud was drawn into studying the mind by his work with **Breuer** on hypnosis and hysteria.

The apparently powerful role played by factors of which patients seemed to be unaware, led Freud to postulate that much of our behaviour is determined by forces that are inaccessible to awareness. Both the id's instincts and many of the super-ego's activities are not known to the conscious mind, but can have its own influence over our opinions and over our desires.

(For further reading Google search: Sigmund Freud.)

The ego is primarily conscious, for it is a metaphor for the psychic systems that have to do with thinking and planning.

But the ego, too, has important unconscious aspects, the defence mechanisms, that protect it from anxiety. Freud considered most of the important determinants of behaviour to be unconscious.

Unlike Freud, I have come to consider the complexities of the mind not through medical practice or psychology or through any academic training, but through years of suffering from my own mysterious wartime memories and trying to understand my own life experience. My experience of this life includes at least one out-of-body-experience, with just a little added interest in reading and research in to the subjects of theology, psychology and philosophy.

However: the *id,* as described by Freud, is present at birth, and provides all the energy needed to fuel the ego and later on, the super-ego. This for me sounds like a very plausible description of the three overlapping dimensions of the mind in life. I agree with Freud and add only that the ego and the super-ego both seem to conspire to repress the original *id,* throughout childhood and through adulthood, simply because both of these states of mind are connected only to the here and now!

That is to say, the *id* was always within me, from day one of this life, and it carries with it all of my past life memories and has feelings and attitudes of its own from the past. However, looking deep into myself, it is not the ego, or my super-ego that is writing this book, but it does rather seem to be the returning *id* that wants to explain itself here. I am saying that if the *id* is the reincarnated soul present at birth, then the ego is that which is the maturing identity with bodily needs and physical desirers, and that the super ego is that mature part of the conscious being that represses the *id*, for the most part of your physical life.

During these years I have obviously come to notice that many of the world's religions include the doctrine that the mind/soul can and does live on, in some form or another after the death of the body, and if that is true, then many people believe as I do, that the mind/soul has no physical link to the earth-bound body.

Out-of-body experiences have been written about and published by people from all nations around the world, usually after having experienced an accident or whilst in hospital on the operating table.

This means that your 'essence of thought' or your ability to think and reason is not powered by any matter or any solid physical form: the personality, the real thinking, analysing, individual *you* can be thrown out of your mortal body during an accident by hard physical impact, by severe pain or apparently by the fear of a painful death!

Many people may instantly revolt against this idea but perhaps one should not. Everybody has the ability to think, reason, calculate, desire, imagine, pretend, daydream, manipulate, visualize and fantasize about erotic liaisons because everybody has a mind capable of doing these things. All of us have this amazing mind from birth and generation after generation we all accept, that is, those people who think about it—that our minds are evolving into something even more powerful than before.

The mind also gives us our complex emotions like love, devotion, envy, jealousy, embarrassment, kindness, guilt, generosity and can ultimately turn us towards aggression, hate, revenge and sometimes towards an immense amount of violence.

So like myself, the curious should want to know exactly where the mind is, what the mind does, how it works and how we can all benefit most from its amazing abilities.

Curiously, the mind (my mind and yours) also has a special way of self-justification which allows us human beings to avoid some guilt by blaming others for actions or inactions, or our personal circumstance for what we have done; equally in the dark ages people blamed evil spirits and demon activity for their wrong doings.

Some people have also been diagnosed by Doctors and Psychiatrists as having dual or multiple personalities. Dual personality disorder, or multiple personality disorder, is apparently caused by some trauma (fear, embarrassment or guilt) in the formative years which causes a splitting of the personality, ultimately generating two or more different identities—or characters. However, if the soul is immortal and continues its journey through time, then some people may well have real multiple personalities inside them which would only need understanding, and possibly combining into one.

We are taught that it is wrong to kill another human being unless we find ourselves involved in a war. Returning troops who have killed mostly avoid feelings of anxiety and guilt because we have this ability to justify our actions, often blaming other people or situations.

If the mind is a naturally evolved mechanism just for the purpose of effortlessly storing memories, information and facts, then the mind should be in harmony with the physical body and help us to stay safe, happy and healthy in a simple but effective manner just like all of the other creatures of the earth. However, that is just not true. The mind actually very often puts us in harm's way and it is not fair to think that it is only exhaustion, intoxication or drug use that makes this happen. Arrogance, Anger, Happiness, Excitement and feelings of great sadness, anxiety, depression, and jealousy can motivate the mortal self into harm's way, and this is just not natural at all!

Drinking alcohol, smoking cigarettes, taking drugs, driving too fast and eating too much food for comfort stimulation or as activity distraction are replacements for purpose, faith, love, affection, achievement or success, and are also, at times, an outward, physical symptom of feeling emotions of inner pain, failure, guilt or stress. We drink and smoke and eat too much unhealthy food as a comforter or for stimulation because we sometimes feel sad, lonely, unappreciated, and unsuccessful, or because we sometimes feel used, abused, insecure, inferior, unsure, lost, or for some just completely confused individuals, just something to while away their time; but surely this sort of thing should not happen. It does not happen to any other animal on the earth unless they have been removed from their natural environment, held captive in a man-made cage and are tormented. **It seems that without God in our lives and**

without a faith in our hearts, mankind only finds unhappiness and insecurity.

Why would something as powerful as a human mind allow a person to damage its own physical being by drinking, smoking, self-harming, driving too fast, or to commit suicide or to kill another person out of anger or jealousy? Surely a powerful mind as we have would only allow its host to conduct its life in a decent, safe and orderly fashion, but no—it does not.

The mind, powerful or not, is (in mortal life) combined with the sensations of the flesh of the body and as such actually needs / even **craves stimulation** from the outside material world, in the form of excitement, affection, adventure, touch, contact, interaction with others and sex; as well as the desire for recognition as a separate and unique identity, and often this seems only to be achieved by dangerous deeds.

It appears to me to be a straight trade-off between the pursuit of happiness and success through adventure that often leads us straight to the same old feelings of failure, of being used and abused, manipulated, hurt, injured or unhappy. In my mind the feeling of depression is the same as feeling unhappy multiplied by a distinct lack of opportunity to find stimulation from the outside (real) world.

Relationships give us stimulation initially. Marriage appears to be an ideal of parental preconditioning; we learn that we should (eventually) pair-off and promise a commitment to another person in return for companionship and joint support of our offspring. Then after some time we do not recognise the benefits of this union, most probably because we also have been led to expect far too much material possession in return for our commitment. This desire for excitement and happiness more often than not these days turns into anger, frustration, resentment and even hatred.

The mind then obviously craves adventure, interaction and stimulation in preference to health, safety and eventual boredom, and again, this is just not known in the animal world from where we came! Very few people can be happy with a sedentary lifestyle and inactivity, yet our immediate ancestors in the animal kingdom can do this.

Bicycle riders, motorcycle enthusiasts, deep-sea divers, mountain climbers, free climbers, parachute jumpers and micro-light flyers to name but a few hazardous hobbyists, all risk serious injury if not death in search of adventure and mind stimulation.

That said, then obviously for most of us anyway, our inner being—our not so righteous decision making, adrenalin hunting individualist mind—is not that afraid of death; but why not? Lately being described as an adrenaline junky, thrill seeking people often have no fear of death!

So could it be possible for the mind to be permanently attached to some sort of different realm?

Whilst thinking about the inner self, it has to be one of the very first and most difficult steps to take—to accept that no-one has yet discovered the true link between the mind and the flesh and blood body. Your brain is flesh and blood and is a mortal biological and physiological device, but the actual home of the mind is not understood—the mind cannot be surgically removed; furthermore, this problem has been much written about and debated many times over through many centuries by some of the best minds in the world, Doctors, Surgeons, Philosophers, Psychologists, Psychiatrists and Therapists alike.

The mind then is a very mysterious thing and this has been a subject of my thoughts many times over. Our DNA and our internal physical structure prove that we are definitely from animal stock; our composition is mostly ape-man or rhesus monkey, as I have been led by my education to understand it. That is why Anthropologists say that we must have evolved slowly over time from animal to mankind.

So it is common knowledge that we are 97/98% animal with an extra special 2/3% mixed in from somewhere else (by the hand of God, or some other Alien Nation's attempts at terraforming and cross breeding) but still as yet unknown source!

Okay, so we are mostly animal, and the point I am trying to make is this, nearly all animals spend their entire days focused on their own physical needs, searching for food, keeping warm and dry, protecting the young and fighting off predators. All of the creatures in the animal kingdom have to be forever focused on the job of providing for their biological needs.

I say that the physiology of our bodies is mostly animal and that is common knowledge worldwide, but, if you analyse how long it takes us to provide for our own daily biological needs, well, it is not very long at all. Washing, shaving, dressing, eating and drinking for a whole day—probably less than fifteen minutes; answering the call of nature, in one whole day—less than ten minutes at the most. So, added up, in one whole day, all of our biological needs take roughly speaking a little less than thirty-five minutes. Okay, but what else are we supposed to be doing with the rest of our days? Looking at the clouds in the sky and pondering on the ways of nature? No, I do not think that evolution has any romantic or artistic notions.

The way of natural evolution has its priorities firmly rooted in survival; therefore I doubt that we humans have come to a point in our own evolution whereby we all have twenty-three hours per day to muse, to ponder, to speculate, to invent and/or in which to write poetry! No, I am thinking that it is no accident that we can provide for our own bodily needs in such a small time, and I do not think it is an accident that our minds can easily be detached from such physiological requirements like the other animals have to, to focus on other subjects like gaining education, understanding, wealth, rewards, security and knowledge.

To my mind and in my understanding of our natural place in the universe I am not surprised that we are supposed to have careers or trades and work forty two hours per week, because I adamantly believe that we have been deliberately engineered to be workers, miners, traders and teachers.
As I already said, evolution has no romantic or artistic notions, and if we evolved from the animal kingdom naturally, then I cannot understand how our **detachable minds** have come in to being!

I think that it would be small-minded indeed to say that the mostly objective, self-analysing thought process struggling for self-survival and the sometimes raw feelings of our emotions that we possess, all interwoven with our memories, are just the by-product of brain-cell activity pursuing the fulfilment of a myriad of physical needs. These needs include warmth, wealth, food, clothing, acceptance, companionship, success and interaction stimuli from the real outside world including the fulfilment of the need to feel loved. Yet there also seems to be a desperate need for some other thing, a separate and individual identity perhaps... philosophers of all ages have referred to this as **the mind-body problem.**

Some narrow-minded people imagine that there are no more mysteries left to explain in this world; however, that statement is simply not true. I find that questions are great motivators for thought—questions like the following: Legally, at what stage does a baby become a person? At what age does a young person become self-aware? At what age does a personality start to form, or is the unique and individual personality immediately present at the moment of conception?

Obviously the answers to these questions are not yet known. However, I am saying that you are a real individual with your unique personality from the very moment of conception, from the very moment that the spiritual form mixes with a physical substance!

However, our young and impressionable minds are deliberately programmed in childhood so that we fit in with our families' ideals, with our community—and society; and therefore many parts of our universal experiences have to be repressed.

We are taught to believe in some things, but not in others—by parental beliefs, by our education, social structure, by our local society, by our chosen religion and by our own research into past religions...

Christianity. A world religion centred on the life and work of Jesus of Nazareth in Israel, and developing out of Judaism. The earliest followers were the Jewish people who, after the death and resurrection of Jesus, believed him to be the Messiah or the long awaited Christ, previously promised by the prophets of the Old Testament. Eternal life is seen as a free gift, made possible through the propitiatory death of Jesus Christ.

All Christians recognise the authority of the Bible, read at public worship, to celebrate the resurrection of Jesus Christ and maintain that the soul, after the death of the body, transmigrates to either Heaven or Hell (i.e. the spirit lives on), or is kept safe to be restored at the physical resurrection of the body in the 'last days'.

The Holy Spirit. A term used to denote the presence or power of God, often imbued with personal or quasi-personal characteristics; in Christian thought considered to be the third person of the Trinity, alongside the Father and the Son. Doctrinal differences exist, though, between Western churches which regard the spirit as 'proceeding from' both the Father and Son, and Eastern Christianity, which accepts procession from the Father only.

In the Bible the spirit was often the vehicle of God's revelatory activity, inspiring the prophets, but it was also depicted as an agent in creation. (*Cambridge Encyclopaedia*, p.575.)

Islam. The Arabic word for 'submission' to the will of God (Allah), the name of the religion originating in Arabia during the 7th century AD through the prophet Mohammed. Followers of Islam are known as Muslims or Moslems, and their religion embraces every aspect of life. The Koran teaches that God is one and has no partners. He is the creator of all things, and holds absolute power over them. All persons should commit themselves to lives of grateful and praise-giving obedience to God, for, on the day of resurrection they will be judged. Those who have obeyed God's commandments will dwell for ever in paradise, (again the spirit lives on) but those who have sinned against God and have not repented will be condemned to an eternity in the fires of Hell.

Spiritualism. An organised religion which believes that spirits of the deceased survive bodily death and can communicate with the living, usually via a medium by means of messages or apparently paranormal physical effects. While many different cultures, past and present, believe in *spiritism* (the ability of spirits of the deceased to communicate with the living), the belief that a person's spirit (including a person's personality and character) can survive after the death of the body and transmigrate persists as a core belief.

Buddhism. A tradition of thought and practice originating in India c.2 500 years ago, and now a world religion, deriving from the teachings of Buddha (Siddharta Gautama), who is regarded as one of the continuing series of enlightened beings.

The teachings of Buddha are summarized in the four noble truths, the last of which affirms the existence of a path leading to deliverance from the universal human experience of suffering. A central tenet is the law of karma, by which good and evil deeds result in appropriate reward or punishment in this life or in a succession of rebirths. It is believed that through a proper understanding of the condition and adherence to the right path, a human being can break the chain of karma. Nirvana, in Buddhism, is the attainment of supreme bliss, tranquillity and purity, when the fires of desire are extinguished, the goal of Buddhists; it is neither personal immortality nor the annihilation of the self, but more like an absorption into the infinite. (*Cambridge Encyclopaedia*, p.855)

Hinduism. The Western term for a religious tradition developed over several thousand years and entwined with the history and social system of India. Common to most forms of Hinduism is the idea of reincarnation and or transmigration. The term *Samsara* refers to the process of birth and rebirth continuing for life after life.

The particular form or circumstances (pleasant or unpleasant) of rebirth are the result of karma, the law by which the consequences of actions within one lifetime are carried over into the next and influence its character. The ultimate spiritual goal of the Hindu is *mohsha,* or release from the cycle of *samsara.*

Past Life Regression. Where a hypnotised person appears to remember past lives sometimes in great detail; adults and children have been known to do this although some psychologists argue that such cases might only represent the person trying to please or impress the hypnotist.

Reincarnation. The belief that following death, some aspects of the 'self' or 'soul' can be reborn into a new body (human or animal), a process that can be repeated many times. This belief is fundamental to many Eastern religions, such as Hinduism and Buddhism, and is also found in more modern Western belief systems such as theosophy. Alleged past-life regressions, where a hypnotized person appears to 'remember' past lives, have recently fuelled Western interest in the possibility of reincarnation, although sceptics suggest that such cases only represent the person trying to meet the wishes or implied demands of the hypnotist. *Cambridge Encyclopaedia*, published 1991, p.1014.

The Holy Ghost or Anti-Matter? It is believed by some that the Holy Ghost is an **existential** (empiric, philosophical theory) divine presence or power, invisible, yet powerful and timeless, proceeding from the Father and the Son; some indeed suggest that it is a procession from the Father only, but could that possibly be a mistranslation? All the answers to my questions could come if that one part of the belief system was a *teeny weeny* mistake and that the scriptures actually really meant to reveal that the Holy Spirit *precedes* the Father and the Son. (Rather than emanating from the Father; or from the Father and Son, it actually precedes them—as in, coming before in time as a separate entity.)

Followers and disciples have believed in, talked about, paid homage to, and worshipped the Father, the Son and the Holy

Spirit (the Holy Ghost) already for thousands of years, quietly accepting the existence of something super-natural, which is, by its very nature, also an invisible and powerful force. I think it strange that science and scientists search tirelessly for anti-matter, that is, the exact opposite of matters-solid-spatial-extension, which also is powerful-invisible and timeless just like the attributes of the Holy Spirit from the ancient and holy scriptures!

It surprises me a very great deal that people actually argue and disagree about the world we live in, in a way much akin to the beliefs of the flat earth society, monism (i.e. any metaphysical doctrine which maintains either that only one thing exists or that only one kind of thing exists = matter.) Parmenides (Ancient Greek Philosopher) denied all plurality whatsoever. Idealists believe that only the mind exists and so everything else is an illusion, i.e. similar to the underlying idea in the film 'The Matrix', and the materialists also only believe that solid matter exists.

From The Cambridge Encyclopaedia: However in Dualism; in one theory of philosophy, any theory which asserts the existence of two different kinds of things; for example, Plato's distinction between temporal things and timeless forms. The most familiar dualism then is between the mind and matter. Descartes (a French rationalist philosopher and mathematician 1596-1650) claimed that matter is substance, whose essence is spatial extension (i.e. mass); whilst the mind or the soul of a being is a non-spatial substance, whose essence is thinking or constructive thought.

Who could possibly live on the Earth, looking up to the stars and the mighty magnitude of the unknown universe above and around us and publicly state having a belief in only one kind of thing... Solid matter... and not believe in a binding force and abstruse (esoteric) energy?

The reasons behind the beginning of the universe is still unknown; the material, or the force binding solids together whilst at the same time, holding them apart, is still an unknown medium. The reason behind mankind's divine creation or natural evolution on this planet is unknown; mankind has not yet travelled into space further than our moon; however, some people are already confident enough to state their concrete belief in only one thing, that is, a belief in only one kind of thing—solid matter!

We still do not know where the universe came from, what started it off, what pushes it forwards, and we do not know what exactly inspires life itself into being, and the more questions we can find to ask, the more questions we have to ask. And the more we should realise just how far we will have to go before we can really understand everything that is real; every way, it is all connected, and we need to understand how things work as a mechanism to create and support life...

I think that I can safely say without criticism that there exists an opposite to everything that we have so far discovered on Earth. Hot-cold, solid-liquid, fast-slow, high-deep and the opposite of alive is dead; but do we really understand the concept of death when almost all civilizations before us have believed in a continual journey of life and death.

The very nature of our spirituality is often viewed just as a romantic notion; it is still unknown or at least not accepted or proved by science. However, our minds have a major carbon-electric make-up, which may not be completely destroyed on death, which could allow for the spiritual personality to continue on a journey of life and death.

Reincarnation is the religious or philosophical concept that the soul or your spiritual self, after biological death, begins a new life in a new body, that may be human, animal or spiritual, depending upon the moral quality of the previous life. This doctrine is a central tenet of the Indian religions—and is the belief that was held by some great historical figures, such as Pythagoras, Plato and Socrates. However, and strangely, it is also a common belief of many other religions such as Druidism, Spiritualism, Theosophy, and Eckankar, and is also found in many tribal societies in such places as Siberia, Africa, North America and Australia.

The word "reincarnation" derives from the Latin, and literally means, "entering the flesh again".
The Greek equivalent roughly corresponds to the English phrase "transmigration of the soul" and also usually implies reincarnation after the death of the body emphasising the continuity of the spirit, not the flesh.

The entire universal spectrum of this belief gives rise to an actual *mechanics of spiritual life,* governing a constant cycle of death and rebirth, governed by karma for both human beings and gods alike, i.e. the Lord Vishnu is accredited for having experienced and lived through ten births and ten lives.

The Celts. Celtic religion also seems to have had reincarnating gods. In the 1st century BC Alexander Cornelius Polyhistor wrote:

The Pythagorean doctrine prevails among the Gauls' teaching that the souls of men are immortal, and that after a fixed number of years they will enter into another body. Julius Caesar recorded that the Druids of Gaul (Britain and Ireland) had metempsychosis (rebirth) as one of their core beliefs.

Philosophical beliefs regarding the existence of an 'unchanging spiritual self' has a definite impact on the romantic ideal of reincarnation and helps to shape our understanding of it. That means we sometimes feel the need to add luck, fate, determinism, yin and yang and/or karma into the cauldron of mixed understanding.

Eternalists choose to believe in an eternal existent spiritual self, comparable to the *atman*, a term used within Jainism to identify the soul. The *atman* survives death and reincarnates as another living being, based upon its karmic inheritance.

The Buddhist concept of reincarnation differs slightly in that that there is no 'eternally surviving soul', but only a stream of consciousness that links one life to the next. However, the very notion of the possibility of reincarnation seems to stem from pre-history and to my mind is linked to the very idea of burying the dead with precious metals, gemstones, spiritual, religious and/or other mystical gifts. It is not a beast without faith that leaves any form of hope, wish, magic or value with a dead body, whether the dead be family, friend or foe. On the contrary, I have to believe that it could only be a solid spiritual faith that was, perhaps even in the very first instance, the actual driving force behind the valuable gifts being buried alongside of the deceased carcase to aid the spirit's journey through the underworld and into the next life.

Taoism. Taoist documents from as early as the Han Dynasty claimed that Lao Tzu appeared on the earth as different people in different times, beginning in the legendary era of Three Sovereigns and Five Emperors. The Chuang Tzu (writings from the 3rd century BC) states that birth is not the beginning; death is not an end. There is existence in between without limitation; there is continuity without a starting point. Existence without limitation is Space. Continuity without a starting point is Time...

This is an excerpt from my book, *The 3 Lives of Peter Miller*, and part of what I can remember:

> ...We have signed the papers and written our names down in capitals, our addresses too, and then we find ourselves at the Train Station.
>
> As the Guard on the Station Platform rings out the first bell we start to take our places in the black trucks behind a dark steam train. There is much crying and wailing from those women and children left behind on the platform, whole families in tears.
>
> There is another bell and suddenly my whole body has gone numb with fear, a shudder under my feet as the train engine starts to come to life. Then there is the high-pitched sound, '*Wheeeee Wheep*' – the long, long whistle

from the Train Engine herself, and now the trucks start shuddering into forward motion underneath of us.

The railway trucks as I remember are timber planks built like cattle sheds on steel carriages with big wheels of iron. The black cattle trucks still have straw and cow dung on the floor and there are no windows and no seats; some of the men force open the side doors and hold them open as we are going along to let some light in and let the bad smell out.

I remember sitting on the floor at the back of the truck contemplating our fate. We have our uniforms on now, long black leather boots with laces up the front pulled through eyelets cut into the leather.

Black trousers, heavy and thick, not sure what material it is but maybe moleskin, long black overcoat, buttoned up and a metal helmet decorated with inter woven metal bands on the front edge above the brim and rather surprisingly with a long metal spike in the middle. (I remember being very concerned about whose side I am fighting for and for what purpose.)

My rifle has a long bayonet with it, clipped underneath to attach to the front end of the rifle for close up work; it has a bolt action mechanism on the right of the barrel and a small magazine underneath which accepts only three bullets; that's next to useless, I remember thinking.

In this cattle truck there are about fifty now uniformed men, all with green backpacks and rifles; some of the men are smoking roll ups, some of the men are full of bravado, being loud and aggressive in gesture and some of the men are scared to death. One man here is visibly shaking.

I am going to fight because it's war and I would not have had a life back home now anyway. I would end up working my whole life just to feed and clothe babies and children, then drink and smoke myself to death because my whole life had gone missing and I could not find a good reason for living anymore.

My memory now is just one of iron train wheels on the track joints, *clackety clacking, clackety clacking,* with the heavy smell of burning coal and hot water being carried along by streams of smoke from the engine up front...

I remember standing up with a wobble on stiff legs, and I have gone over to the door of this cattle truck and a smoking man throws the last stub of his smoke through the door and makes way for me to see.

Looking back down the track at the long line of black trucks, I see they are all the same, being towed along the tracks and being flanked in the East by a huge dark mountain range.

Twenty-five black trucks all-in-all, fifty uniformed men in each truck, that's one thousand two hundred and fifty men going to war, all towed along by one steam engine...

The trucks are all black, painted black (I think) in preparation for the war; someone's been employed rubbing out the name of the engine and the numbers of the trucks.

The train journey is a long one and an emotional one; it takes several days to reach our destination.

Then after disembarking, there is the marching, six abreast at first, rifles slung over our shoulders and all these men marching in unison. I can hear the stamp, stamp, stamp of their feet in polished black boots going onwards together, perhaps towards our final resting place with each soldier wearing his pointy tin hat!

There are horses being whipped in the road because they cannot pull their cartloads of supplies and ammunition through all of the mud and the noise of cannon fire is growing louder and more constant as we are drawing nearer.

Rows of soldiers all wearing black, six abreast, across this cobbled road become four abreast; then one day later we become two abreast until we are crawling through the front line trenches in France of the First World War. This place I believe to be The Western Front and I ended up in Cambrai, stomping through the thick mud carrying my heavy rifle, then crawling on all fours, getting closer and closer to the front, peering through firing holes looking just for a glimpse of the enemy and then, most probably, death for us all.

It is raining very heavily. We are all cold and wet with shells exploding nearby, horses and carts now replaced by the roaring and the rattling of Iron Tanks and we are repairing the wooden trench shorings, digging holes for the latrines, digging out by hand deep bunkers for the Officers' Quarters, shorn up with wooden planks and lit by smoky metal Tilley lamps that burn night and day.

Even the Officers' Hole is no place to be for mortal man.

Then I am digging again, more trenches and quietly we are moving closer and closer towards the nasty greengrocers and the deadly newsagents and tobacconists who were most probably digging their trenches just as hard and fast and doing and thinking just the very same things as I was doing on this side of the front line.

At night our troops go out and set up rows and rows of barbed wire across the front line so the enemy forces cannot easily charge at us, but then I know their men are doing exactly the same thing. Now I remember the screaming, the men dying, the bits of men's bodies, bloody severed arms and legs, strewn amongst the dead and the dying, blood over my trench coat from somebody's head being blown off by a cannon shell.

I also remember the head lice, the biting and the scratching that almost sent you mad with frustration and the metal tanks stuck in the muddy pits, the cannon fire; the noise was such that our eardrums burst and some of the men had blood running down their necks!

I could not hear what men were shouting at me. I remember, there was so much noise and the cleats of the tanks tracks clink and squeal as the metal parts try to move with sharp stones trapped between them and the smoke gets in your eyes, which is good for some, covering up the fact that they are actually crying, uncontrollably with fear.

Planks of timber for shoring up the trenches are sawn up into wooden pads and strapped to the tanks' tracks to help keep them out of the muddy bogs but this is ineffective.

Then on another day there is a moment's peace, ten or fifteen minutes with no exchange of fire at all and it stops raining and the sun shines and someone is milking a dairy cow for milk for the Officers' tea. "Oh, one just cannot fight a war without milk in one's tea," said our captain whilst laughing and probably going mad himself with fear. Sadly we do not get tea, not the infantrymen— we have water in our hip flasks. The fighting men get more dry bread biscuits and more gruel, more over stewed vegetables with loads of water and no meaty bits.

Now I remember being shouted at because my boots are covered in mud. The Corporal, who is 'a horrible little man' appears to be so cross with me...

He is shouting at me, even screaming at me to clean the mud off of my boots, yet I know very well that he is acting this way through fear of his own life, probably not knowing what else he can do to save himself except to put other men down, presumably boosting his own ego, instead of breaking down and losing it completely.

The Corporal is a wafer thin man, a stick insect with a black moustache and a twisted ugly face with a short but stout stick held under his arm which he uses to hit his men with when he gets terribly annoyed; he also wears a metal cross around his neck held on a black leather thread. "Tend to your boots man!" he spits in my face again. "Tend to your boots, you horrible little man, don't you know there's a war on!" I remember thinking that this man's mind must be as ugly as his face is, and that thought then, even now, is completely embedded into my memory.

I am undoing my laces, pulling them out of their eyelets, cleaning the mud from my boots, then re-lacing them up again; re-threading them is a time-consuming business as these boots come up to my knees, but then, within the space of one day the Corporal is on my case again... He is shouting and spitting in my face: "Tend to your boots, man! Tend to your boots!"

But there is mud everywhere. Planks of wood and pallets have been laid in the bottom of the trenches to walk on, but even these planks sink into the mud. It rains almost every day and the beasts of burden (mules) that bring in the ammunition and food supplies just make more mud. Then, in-between bouts of fighting, men casually roll cigarettes and lean against the muddy banks, absorbed in a moment of distraction. I am smoking tobacco too, and thinking about the thin metal spike on the top of our helmets and I am wondering what exactly it is meant for.

The spikes on top of our helmets are an issue for me and even cause me anxiety for some strange reason. (I cannot accurately remember why this was.) Perhaps I really did have some doubts about which side I was fighting for...

Now I am up the bank, and pointing my rifle through a firing hole underneath of the barbed wire, looking for the enemy; we are all keeping a watchful eye because some of the troops are going to creep out at night and throw hand grenades into the enemy trenches, into their underground bunkers and their machine gun positions. More shopkeepers and more steel workers, farriers and postmen are going to have their heads and arms blown off by these crude devices.

This rifle is a mystery to me also. (It was in my past life and still is a mystery to me today.) It is supposed to be the best of modern technology (in 1917), a most modern invention designed for war, yet it only has a magazine attached for three more bullets. Who designed this magazine, an idiot?

Even I know that six more bullets would be better than three, and by the very same token, ten more bullets could easily be pushed down a magazine against a wire spring. So, I have issues with the design of my rifle as well as having issues with the spike on top of our helmets and with wilfully trying to kill innocent men!

I do not really want to throw grenades into a trench full of innocent men. I do not want to shoot bullet holes through innocent men, nor do I wish to run them through with my bayonet; but I will; when that time comes I will shoot to kill because this is war; it's a war without a purpose except for one man's arrogant pig-headed ego, who puts thousands of men to death and starves the working classes and the children of his own country.

Still, now there is a moment of peace, the sun shines down on us and the mood of the men is momentarily lifted. The supplies are coming in on the backs of the mules and being equally distributed amongst the men and I am given more tobacco, papers, a tinder box and a newspaper. But, it is not a new newspaper, it is days old and one with muddy fingerprints and the ink is smudged in places. Some of the pages are torn, but still, the great man on the front page is now an item of ridicule and hilarity, but here in the trenches I do not understand why!

Did I ever get the joke or have I just lost that part of my memory? No, thinking about that, I do not think that I ever understood the joke because I believe it was one of Irony. One King is dead—Archduke-Franz-Ferdinand is dead, is that not enough?

Now these men want to make a fool out of another who sends his men to their deaths—something that is not in my sense of humour; however it does seem very funny to some of these men with their pointy metal helmets on their heads and their very muddy boots.

For some reason, **a photograph is taken of the men in the trenches.** I am also photographed. I am in the middle of a line-up of about twelve soldiers. A photographer has a camera hidden inside of a wooden box held steady upon a tripod of sticks and metal hinges. I remember the photographer also wears a silly hat but it is not like ours—it's not made of metal, it is made of stiff fabric and has a wide brim. The flashlight goes off leaving a thin trail of smoke and a strange smell in the air like matches or burning magnesium.

All these things I remember just as if it was a couple of years back, but it was not a couple of years ago; from today, it was nearly one hundred years ago, so how can I possibly remember it?

The 3 Lives of Peter Miller continues on, recalling the very moment of his death and then his rebirth as Peter Miller (P.M/M.P.). (Peter Miller is obviously myself.)

But I wish to leave my memories right there for the moment; yet I wonder if the picture that was taken of myself and another eleven Prussian Soldiers in the front line trenches was ever published in a newspaper?

If it was published, then it still might be found today. In 1916/1917 there could not have been very many pictures taken deep in the trenches of the central forces front line in 1916/1917.

I might one day be able to look at a photograph of myself, a photograph that was taken ninety-six years ago.

CHAPTER FIVE

As a matter of fact our Minds are very powerful. Everybody should be aware by now that positive thoughts are better for a person's physical and mental well-being than negative thoughts—having a positive feeling, perhaps love for someone, a liking for someone or a liking for something such as a pet, all of which is much better for you than feeling any distrust, dislike, anger, hatred or jealousy.

I love my children and very much hope that they also love me; for my part I believe that love is the first most important emotion that we can feel and give to our young. Love and devotion for our own creation constitutes the absolute foundation of Fatherhood.

We human-beings have a fascination about understanding the feeling of love, of finding and feeling and expressing the feeling of love towards another human-being. Feeling loved or loving someone else has the very same positive affect on our mental and physical well-being!

Liking the actual Street where you live, being good friends with the neighbours and loving the house where you live is much better than hating or despising it. Loving your job, feeling love towards your partner and your children is exactly the same thing. It provides us all with happiness, a sense of joy, a real purpose for being alive and often that much needed inner peace.

Believing in a Supernatural being or believing in a **Creator God / or in the Holy Father,** should then have the very same effect. It should benefit anyone who has the desire or the inclination to feel better about this world and increase their own feeling of self-worth, inner peace and daily happiness. However not everybody of every nation believes in God; in fact, the numbers of true believers are falling. Many still do though. Although some now think having any belief in a God, or in any form of religious faith, to be at the least foolhardy and at worst downright stupid, yet the benefits of loving something, anything or everything and anywhere are obviously far more beneficial than doubting or hating.

Firstly. I am a Dualist: a believer in many things rather than a believer in just one thing. (Could that be Pluralist?) I cannot just believe in the material combination of solid matter when often solids are not solid and water is not a solid. I have to believe that more than one kind of thing exists in this world at the same time.

I believe that matter has some kind of **spatial extension** (it uses up and fills a measurable amount of space), but that its opposite, anti-matter/earth energy/Earth Spirit if you prefer, does not have any spatial extension, but is a completely opposite substance to the former, is invisible, shapeless, odourless and is in fact a timeless form. Anti-matter or Earth's Energy, whatever, is very much like an immense cloud of electrical force that you cannot be aware of unless you are out-of-your-body, which is the exact opposite of everything we understand as being real.

So I am a **spiritualist also**, because I believe it takes more than one kind of thing to make life possible, i.e. at least three things are required, the complex structure of physical matter, some form of liquid, and differential electrical forces. I believe that the mind is your soul and your psyche, and also that, based on my own memory of what **out-of-body** experience feels like, your soul can survive in some form or another after your bodily death, and that it can dissipate, transmigrate (move about) and reincarnate elsewhere, depending upon your spiritual strengths and your personal understanding... If I did not completely believe in these different things, the matter and the anti-matter, (physical form and spiritual energy), I am sure that I would feel very isolated, very lonely and very unimportant indeed, and even more importantly... I would not have been able to choose to come back to life.

Many years ago, somebody told me, or tried to explain to me that the human heart had a hole in it, an empty part where the true love of God used to be, but now is sadly missing and the heart of man is left lonely and wanting. Well, for my own reasons I have been considering that statement for a very long time along with my other concerns and I have decided that it is not a true statement. Describing the feelings of the heart is wrong for a start because all thoughts, feelings, loves and desires are the sole domain of the human mind, not the heart. And it is not a reference to something missing in our minds either. I believe we all still have all that which we started out with, but the fact is that we now actually have something else, something unnatural. To the way I think about my own mind it would seem that we have an ability to detach our focus from the day-to-day physical needs of the body and let the mind wander where it may or for it to be easily distracted. Our minds somehow have a freedom that other animals and Apes of the earth do not. Is this why human beings find so much comfort from inconsequential and often stupid things such as gold and silver jewellery, shiny tokens and trinkets, dummies, dollies and other body adornments? (Tattoos included in this!)

In many ways it seems that we can turn off our minds from our natural day-to-day realistic physical needs and fantasies and to soul search (self-analyse), to ponder on other things, which is why we can sometimes feel, cold, lonely, lost and insecure. Unlike our counterparts in the animal world, our minds are relatively discontented with the physical world, and this is because our minds can now somehow reach out beyond the physical body and we can expect much, much more than just the practical, the down to earth and the most basic of necessities...

The reality of our lives is often cold, hard and lonely; however, to believe in something supernatural, spiritual, scientific or political or not to believe in anything except personal needs, is a birth right, and should remain a birth right. Whether or not to decide for oneself what is right and what is wrong, what exists and what does not exist, should always remain a personal preference and I would never wish to change that!

For many obvious reasons some people grow weary of this life, and others suffer so badly throughout that many might prefer just to let go after death and just dissipate through the universe and never want to live again!

However, I remember that when I was dead, I could not so easily rest. Firstly, somehow my mind would not let go, taking on a unique power of its own; secondly, I could not even control my mind to rest: it would have no part in my ambition to let go and, thirdly, the noise of the grass growing through my corpse and the wind rushing through my mind was **enough to keep the Devil awake...**

Scientists will one-day admit that they cannot possibly explain everything about the human consciousness or the infinite mechanisms of the universe to us, simply because our perspective of it is far too narrow and far too flat. For the majority of human-beings we are just far too far away from anything interesting to even be bothered...(because we live on the very edge of the known universe).

But then obviously we know that since the very beginning of our time on this earth, many people have written accounts of the Angels coming down to the Earth from Heaven. Gods and Star people have been seen, conversed with, and drawn and written about since the very beginning of our time! ...People of many civilizations have even 'conceptualized' what Heaven is and where it is (obviously on top of Mount Olympus) and cavemen to renascence artists have created pictures and descriptions of this most Heavenly place.

People have learnt about fortune telling, tarot cards, extra-sensory perception, casting spells and incantations, spiritualist and mediums and exorcisms (that is, to dispossess evil spirits). Some believe they can communicate with the dead and some have even believed in the art of witchcraft as most of us now believe in the power of positive thought. Some to a greater or lesser extent have accepted these kinds of supernatural abilities. As a race of beings we have always seemed to want to be more special than we really are, or is it that we are so very much more special than we think we are, simply because we have forgotten the truth...? A very long time ago the American Indians lived in harmony with nature, with no newspapers, no cars, no telephones, just a direct connection to the natural world, and yet they believed that the soul lived on in the ground or in the wind or in the mountains after the death of the body. So do the Hindu and the Buddhists as did the Inca and the Aztec civilizations, and also before them, the early Egyptians and the Sumerians from Mesopotamia.

Christianity prefers a more conservative view and prefers to suggest that the soul only migrates to Heaven or to Hell depending upon your deeds and your failings in this one lifetime—or more accurately, depending on your acceptance of Jesus Christ and his love to freely forgive or pardon your failings or transgressions.

Now we live in a Great Society with doctors, and surgeons, science, chemistry, medicine, modernization, mobile phone technology, industrialisation, mass marketing, media, motorways, air-travel and politics, package holidays and satellites orbiting the planet. We are now looking forward to space travel to different stars and to seek out new planets (for terraforming) for us to **make habitable for ourselves to live on.**

So as a Race of beings we like to think of ourselves as intelligent and that we only believe in actual real solid fact, but the real truth may be that we have forgotten the truth about who we really are or we have been deprived of the knowledge of what we really are...

In this western world when you feel ill you visit the doctor, and for one reason or another one day your doctor might prescribe a placebo, a course of tablets which contain nothing but sugar. However, it has been scientifically proven by research and the analysis of data, that some people do benefit from this course of tablets simply because the patient is told to, and really believes that they will help. The mind and what it believes has a very great influence upon the health of your whole physical and mental being!

On the surface of our society I believe, or at least I can imagine, that through the eyes of children, most grown-ups appear to be happily occupied with the complexities of their own private lives—whether busy, happy or sad, whether working or not, successful or not, and on the whole they appear to be quite sane. However, thirty, forty, fifty-something years later with the advantage of years of experience, and it becomes strikingly obvious that we grown-ups are not at all sane.

In fact, for some it is quite the opposite—because actually we human-beings are not completely all-right and some in particular appear at the very least, a little bit crazy, self-centred, self-important, insecure, jealous homicidal maniacs. And that would be a very close description of some.

In general people are a miss-mash of complicated desires, confusing emotions, partly emotionally repressed, with faults, failings and fears, with insecurities, greed and imprinted knee jerk reactions.

But why is this when we should be so fantastically great! But then I imagine that this happens very easily because all of our childhood experiences are different; our parents are different and all of our grandparents were different, and through every generation in the Western world the spirits of children are deliberately repressed (children 'should be seen but not heard').

And to further compound this damage, **there is no school, college or university** which adequately offers education in, or degree courses in the truth of human evolution, for learning what 'normal human behaviour' is, or what human spirituality is!

Or is there? ... I have only recently discovered the schools of Esoteric thought! (I recommend the reader to Jonathan Black's *The Secret History of the World*.)

...For those interested in Esoteric philosophy (school of ancient arts and understanding) the greatest miracle always was the human consciousness... Scientists have always been fascinated by the extraordinary series of balances between various sets of necessary factors, that have been more than just necessary but crucial, in order to make this life on this earth, possible. They talk in terms of balances between heat and cold, wetness and dryness, the earth being so far from the sun but not any further away, the sun being at a particular stage of its own evolution and not burning up.

But then looked at from the point of view of esoteric philosophy, we can now see that an equally extraordinary series of balances has been required to make our subjective consciousness what it is, or to put it another way, it is truly amazing that the mind has the perfect structure and balance that it has!

What possibly is there inside of our mind that makes it possible to have a continuous internal story line of self-awareness, that awareness of experience—the internal narrative-thing that we verbally write in our heads every day and all day, resulting in our conscious perception, our understanding of ourselves and our relevant position in our society and as a human-being...? Of course, it is a concept only allowed to happen by the fantastic ability to remember every detail.

If I could not remember what I did yesterday or the day before that, then I would not be very able to decide what I need to be doing today or tomorrow. If I could not remember where I lived, I could not return to my home, and if I could not remember my childhood, I would not know how to bring up my own children better!

The point about my memory is this: I have an amount of acquired (and more to the point, *required*) memory that I can access on a daily or weekly basis. I remember most things that I need to, but not everything; if I remembered every single detail of my life I would never be able to sleep at night for all the ordering, understanding, cross examining and filing away that goes on when I want to go to sleep. I can remember the most important things, like where I go, what I did, what I said and what I want to do tomorrow, plus the dates through the year of which are important to me.

Thus, when I retire to bed, it doesn't usually take too long to understand what I did, what was said to me, what it meant to me and what I must do tomorrow.

In other words, I can remember what I want to do now, but at the same time I can also remember a very long list of the other things that I need to do later, which is also listed in an order of urgency.

Other checks and balances are necessary in order for me to think freely for myself and to weave the desires of my conscious mind around the personality of my inner being. Perceptions and emotions and irritations and fantasises are regularly reigned in at particular points to allow me to continue to do what I must do.

I perceive that for most of us life is a struggle and the world can be cold and hard; however, although sometimes I might feel a little depressed about it, I do not cry about it. Instead, occasionally if I walk past a beggar on the street I might give him one or two pounds or buy a *Big Issue* and that may be enough to correct my own sadness at the cruelty of the world. I guess that I salve my conscience with a token of charity.

The point being that you cannot grieve continually over something sad or bad for infinity and you cannot be so callous as to laugh hysterically at somebody else's grief for eternity either. There are built-in mental checks and balances, boundaries and freedoms which expand and constrict at times for you to survive grief and check arrogance, and all this seems to be intentionally built-in.

We also have freedoms to choose what we want to think about; obviously we think about our physical desires as they rise up into our conscious thoughts, like warmth, shelter, companionship, food and drink and the desire for sex, but there is more, so much more. Like the desire to climb up a tree or climb up a mountain just to get a better picture of our surroundings, which also seems to be inbuilt into a human-being; but we can also choose to concentrate on different subjects, and sometimes difficult subjects, if it pleases us to do so; this entertains us and often delivers solutions to problems which annoy us!

If I did not have the freedom to choose what I thought about, then I would just be an animal, just like a Chimpanzee or like one of my cats, which only seems to think about its natural physical needs and its immediate environment. If I did not have **the freedom to choose** what I think about, perhaps I would obsess over the best food all day, be tied to my job or to the kitchen sink, or to worrying about my children obsessively, or I might become neurotic about other unimportant and irrelevant things.

But no, I have the freedom to focus my mind on problems, ambitions, projects, desires and sometimes on wild fantasies instead of just obsessing over my immediate physical needs or my family's immediate housing needs...

Somewhere along our line of natural evolution or our unnatural development we have produced in our minds not only the obvious abeyance to our bodily needs, and the ability to objectively consider things. However, at will we can change the subject of thought, and even to choose to forget that line of thought altogether and move our focus of concentration to other areas unrelated to anything immediately necessary.

The mind of an animal, wild or domesticated, cannot do that. Animals are tied to their own daily physical needs and to the needs of their social structure; but our own minds are not tied to our physical needs but seem to be tied instead, somehow, to our emotional state, or our desired emotional state instead!

To explain that: we can plan ahead, well into the future, to bring about some personal success which will make us happier and or wealthier in the future, i.e. I do not actually want to sit here at my desk every Saturday and Sunday for six months writing this book—it takes too much of my free time away from my family, takes a great deal of concentration and after a while sitting down I get cramp in my legs and in my feet which I do not like. However, and going back to my mind somehow being tied to my desired future emotional state, I do want to publish this book; it is my story, I want other people to be able to see it, read it, to enjoy it and to own it, and in six months' time it will make me very happy indeed. ...So, in my mind and my own thoughts about myself, I have considered my place in this world and worked out that I will be happier in the immediate future if I commit myself to the task and sit down and write this book, and that is **objective thought.**

Obviously, I am trying to say that our free thinking minds are a miracle, and along with this is fantastic ability to be aware of the self and motivate the body to seek shelter and sustenance; but it can also concentrate, reason, work out, desire and manipulate numbers, questions, solve problems, and it can also consider its physical and mental well-being in the future.

My memory of the events of my life and my previous lives makes me the person that I am today and that is precisely right for all human-beings. I was born in a house in the Kent countryside, grew up on a smallholding with cats, dogs, a cow, several Toggenburg goats, Rode Island Red Chickens and a pack of very white geese. My very first job I had after leaving school was working on a mixed farming Estate where I drove agricultural tractors, and was taught how to plough fields, cultivate crops, bale hay and occasionally 'riddle' potatoes. If my childhood and if my youth and if my memories of that experience were any different, then it would be impossible to be myself or even know myself.

So, my personality, my individual way of understanding about this world and my spiritual beliefs entwined, provide me with my objective view of reality and my consideration, and my passion and my compassion for life. The thing is, our memories are so very vital for everybody. So then, **why would my mind, when I was only a very small child,** create such a massive amount of very exact and detailed memories, replete with colour and noise about previous lives in different countries, if I never had them?

And this is exactly my very point. I do remember my previous lives because I can decide which bits to remember, stop there, rewind to my very beginning or fast track to the end of it and these memories are always the same. That is because they are real memories etched onto my very soul for all time...

Yes, you can say that my childhood in this life was a rather negative experience, but my father was no worse than anybody else's and he was clever enough to have built our house with his own hands, and we had land, animals and apple trees. I might have been misunderstood, but I was never particularly cold, hungry or insecure. Many children I am sure would have willingly swapped their experience for mine, so again, why would my mind create such a fantasy that I believe I could remember obviously from before being born here!

For many years I was side-tracked if not completely derailed by my parents and my immediate family's attitude to their facts about this life. I was encouraged not to bother with the bigger questions about life. Why are we here? What exactly are we? Where do we come from? More to the point, why am I still here? And, what exactly is on the other side of the known universe?

"No more questions," Dad would say, "Go and dig over the vegetable patch, go and mow the lawn or go and rake the drive flat! Do something useful, anything rather than question the world." Talk about having a false reality forced upon you!

But my previously repressed spirit has obviously now decided that it is the right time to emerge and to tell my own story—

or to allow it to reveal itself—and I will try as best I can to explain how it works, at least for one good reason—to redress the balance of what my life should have been about **rather than just doing what was generally expected...**

The mind and lying. When I was a child I might have lied to my Mother about how much pocket money I had left or I might have lied when I absolutely denied any part of eating all of the chocolate biscuits from her special tin. When I was a teenager I might have lied to one girl or another about my feelings of love, when all I felt (for some) was lustful desire. Later on I might have lied to my employer about my health when I phoned in sick, but spent the day in Eastbourne on the beach with my girlfriend; but in all my years I have never lied to myself and I don't think that it would even be possible!

What point would it make and what good would it do to tell myself a lie? Yes, it would be pointless, if not ludicrous; in fact, to lie to yourself would probably pre-empt some form of madness. After all, I know when I am in love, I know when I am happy, sad, hungry, bored, tired, randy, or when I feel ill, so how can I lie to myself? If I did not have another life, if I was not a German soldier, and if I cannot remember that boy's mother baking bread when I was that other kid, then my mind has lied to me... and for why?

Somehow I see the world in a mind before matter way, obviously, or to my mind anyway, you must be some form of energy before you are born, because if you are born as matter without energy you would not be able to breathe or open your eyes or operate in any way. So somewhere along the line I must have had some spark of energy which must then have manifested itself into my physical form. My point being if I am energy first; if I am thought first; if I am mind first, then it would not be the end at the moment of bodily death. I am 'that which I am' and will do all that I will do, because I can think things through, remember who I am and feel my emotional states, and all of this, not because I was fortunate to be born with arms, legs and a head, so I am myself (thought/spirit self) first and a human-being second.

Obviously I am saying all this purely because I easily remember former lives. If I could not remember such things then I would be writing about construction and civil engineering because that would be all I would have known. At the end of the day you will have to decide for yourself if I am telling you the whole truth or not.

However, there is far more to this story than the romantic notion of having an immortal soul. For one thing, as I wrote in *The 3 Lives of Peter Miller,* both previous lives were in service because it seems that he/I never had any choice in the matter—it was serve or starve. Both of my former lives were in every sense wretched, pointless, cold and hungry, frustrated by head lice and malnutrition and in both cases rapidly followed by a premature death. Hardly a romantic or comforting tale either to invent for oneself or remember in actual truth.

When I felt like I was flying down to earth rather like a bird on the wind, perhaps I should have landed in India; the Buddhist tradition would probably render my story uneventful, even trivial, seeing as most Indian people accept reincarnation as completely natural and the Buddhist way is to teach about a path of enlightenment which eventually may stop the continuous cycle of life and death.

I refer the reader to *The Secret History of the World* by **Jonathan Black. Chapter 3 (page75).**

If you could remove the sympathetic nervous system from the body of a man and stand it up on its own, it would look very much like a tree. I could not possibly guess how or why this is but it is true.

Kabbalistic or Esoteric thought all over the ancient world is concerned with the subtle energies which flow through and around this very vegetable looking part of the body and also with the 'flowers' of this enigmatic tree. The flowering regions upon this tree are called *chakras* which the ancients believed operated as organs of perception. The great centre of this seemingly vegetable core of the nervous system of the human body feeds on the waves of light and warmth radiating from the sun, and is called the chakra of the solar plexus or 'solar plexus' because it is formed in this area. Awareness and acceptance of this vegetable element of the human body remains greatest among the people of China and Japan. In Chinese medicine the energetic flow of this life force is called *chi*, and is understood to animate the body, and disease arises when this delicate network of energies becomes blocked. (See Black, p. 76.) The fact remains however that this flow of energy is still undetectable by modern science and must somehow operate in some unknown realm between the human spirit and the physical mass of the animal body, and does not make the medication any less effective as generation upon generation attest.

The organs belonging to this vegetable body are situated in nodes up and down its trunk and made up of a different number of petals, the solar plexus chakra for example having ten petals... The Pineal gland is a small greyish gland about the size of an almond, which is situated in the brain where the spinal cord reaches up into it. In esoteric philosophy, when we have an idea, our pineal gland begins to vibrate, and, if spiritual discipline is used to increase and prolong this vibration, this may lead to the opening of the third eye, situated in the middle of the forehead.

(Incidentally, I refer the reader to *The 3 Lives of Peter Miller* and the rattling of hazel nuts in a paper bag. Chapter One, page 23.)

Moving on: *The Secret History of The World* (Chapter 7, page 137):

When HERODOTUS was puzzling over the strange wooden statues of the kings who had ruled over the world before any human king, the Egyptian priests told him that no-one could understand this history without learning about 'the three dynasties'. If HERODOTUS had been an initiate of the Mystery Schools he would have known that the three dynasties were, first, the oldest generation of creator gods: Saturn, Rhea and Uranos. The second generation was made up of Zeus, his siblings and their children—such as Apollo and Athena—and lastly the generation of demi-gods and heroes such as Hercules, Theseus and Jason...

In the tales of Hercules we can see how human the man-gods where becoming. Hercules wanted to be left alone to get on with his life of enjoying all the earthly pleasures—but he was repeatedly interrupted by his duty to follow his spiritual destiny (just like me). A stumbling, bungling, sometimes laughable figure, Hercules was torn between the two opposing cosmic forces of Earth and the spiritual world... Hercules was hag-ridden by desire for Deianira.

The twelve labours of Hercules show him moving through a series of trials, each one set for him by successive spirits who rule the constellations. It is a series of trials which all demi-gods must take, and by and large they take to these trials unwittingly, just like Hercules. The life of Hercules then, illustrates to all of mankind the pains of being human. He is every man, trapped in a continuous cycle of pain and desire! (Adapted from page 146.)

From *The Secret History of the World* by Jonathan Black. Continue (from page188):

There is an extraordinary saying, attributed to Meister Eckhart, the thirteenth-century German Mystic: 'If you fight your death, you'll feel the demons tearing away at your life, but if you have the right attitude to your death, you will be able to see that devils are really angels setting your spirit free.'

And he goes on to say... An initiate of a secret society develops the right attitude to death.
He sees behind appearances and knows that demons in their proper place perform an invaluable role in what might be

called the 'ecology' of the spirit world... What the initiate of Secret Societies would be taught was not in any way academic as such, but would have been existential, i.e. real.

As I now understand it, in Athens the Ancient Greek initiate and/or the Ancient Egyptian initiate at Luxor (i.e. beginner of spiritual learning) would, through the use of prescribed drugs and intoxicants, religious chants calling on the spirits of the dead and snake pits, be literally scared out of his own skin. In other words the initiate would be taught through fright out-of-body experience! (Page190.)

As I have been saying all along, once you have been aware of your own spiritual self outside of the body, then you know for an actual fact that you have no need of the physical form and therefore, no need to fear death.

In the ancient mystery texts, initiates were taught the very secret names of the spirits that guard the entrance to every sphere, and sometimes, too, secret handshakes and other signs and formulae needed to successfully negotiate for entry therein. In the *Pistis Sophia*, these spheres are envisaged as made of crystal and the entrance keepers of these spheres as archons or demons. In all of the ancient religions, the being who guides the human spirit through the underworld and helps him to negotiate the way past guardian demons is the god of the planet Mercury.

CHAPTER SIX

Just mythology—or the real understandings of the Ancient Egyptians? (Much of the following discussion has been inspired by a reading of Egyptian *Mythology* by Richard Patrick. Octopus Books, 1972)

An interesting thought about the Ancient Egyptian civilization which has just occurred to me, (this is me and not from the abovementioned book!) these very ancient people used to write with pictures hand carved in stone (called hieroglyphs); they used whole rows of pictures to convey their ideas, messages and about their social structure and the work of their gods, culminating in the whole story of their history and their belief systems being told down through the generations throughout all time. However, we in today's world use word combinations starting in a sentence, then in paragraphs to convey a picture, an idea or a series of pictures and a series of ideas which culminate in the story of our history, our social structure and our present-day belief systems.

…Five or more thousand years of evolution, just to alter our method of trying to explain some of the very same, strange things about this world and about our nature, but just in a different way?

The Ancient Egyptian paintings, drawings and carvings always had an absolute abundance of flying birds with human faces and gods depicted with wings of which we today instantly acknowledge as our ancient ancestors' attempts to explain the spiritual journeys of souls passing through the underworld before returning to life. To all of the ancient cultures of our world, the dead were not acknowledged as being lost for ever, but were believed to be continuing their natural, forward journey after the soul was released!

...Yet, here I am, five thousand years later trying to explain the very same belief in spiritual journeys through the underworld to the afterlife with my very own words and prompted to do so only because I remember my own past-lives. However, in my mind, passing through the underworld or journeying through the spiritual world is just a precursor to arriving in the Afterlife, which is back on the earth's surface again and again!!

If I can remember previous lifetimes, and other people have reported that they can remember previous lifetimes, then something more than natural mortal life and death is occurring here. I cannot say that this 'something more' is in any way a 'supernatural ability' because it might be the most 'natural' thing in the world for a human to do, if only we just knew it.

Working on the farm I saw with my own eyes that the body of any mammal can be stillborn, stiff and lifeless, right at the start of its experience; and when we die, however we die, our bodies become lifeless. So, my point obviously is that there must be something else needed. Some sort of spark of energy or spiritual form that allows the animation of the body, and it is this energy, this spirit within, that I believe the ancient Egyptians were trying to explain right through their whole afterlife belief system!

It seems to me at least that all the people of the ancient world developed a conceptual belief in real mythological beings, monsters and demons and described actual layers and structures of the spirit world, which should have a great effect on our opinions about their knowledge of spirituality.

Where did ancient man learn about life after death? Was it just fantasy born out of the fear of death? Were they told by their gods or were they so much closer to nature that they all remembered previous existences? Is it impossible for the soul to survive and reincarnate, or have we just forgotten something very important about the true nature of mankind and now only consider ourselves to be mortal?

These mythological tales, described by all of the ancient peoples from different and very isolated cultures around the world, should in turn affect how we understand our own spirituality.

Obviously, I am by no means an expert on the Ancient Civilizations of our world, but I do profess to understand exactly what they were trying to describe.

However, I am very sure that some of our world's Archaeologists would state that at the very least, the Ancient Civilizations of upper and lower Egypt, which were the world's very **first ever monument building people,** believed in life after death...

The way the early Egyptian people understood this world is strange indeed. They were not only, most probably, the very first civilization on the earth, but the first to start the pyramid building program. There are around ninety-four pyramid structures in Egypt. They also manufactured massive edifices and entities above the ground—monumental carvings of their kings. And then constructing just as much under the ground in their labyrinths and tombs chiselled out of solid stone and even more curiously, they were building exactly in the very centre of our world's land mass. Was that by accident or coincidence, and does that fact have any spiritual significance? They also had some very strange but connected ideas because they coveted (desired, sought-after, looked forward to) death and an afterlife, far more than life itself!

It seems this expectation of an afterlife was somehow 'hardwired' into their understanding of their nature; their mortal life in one body was expected to be only a short, yet transitory state, allowing some precious time in which to prepare for the Afterlife! And as far as I understand it, every Ancient Egyptian, regardless of rank or position, desired to be mummified at death and so secure his or her place in the afterlife. So why was mummification so important?

They somehow decided to believe that if their body was preserved with bitumen, oils and spices and all wrapped up as a classical mummy, the resulting preservation of the body possibly for ever was enough to secure the survival of the spirit! It all points to their belief that if the body did not decay naturally and not dissipate, then the spirit of the dead would someday return to restore their body for another life.

The Afterlife was of great importance to them and few people have ever since devoted so much of their time and their wealth to the preparation for their death than they did. From the moment of his accession, a king would start to plan and to build his tomb and the funerary temple attached to it, where his individual spiritual being was to be perpetuated after his death. Eventually there were a great wealth of officials and commoners alike, to a more or lesser degree, who worked hard and hoarded to provide for themselves and other family members suitable funerary equipment, to pay for the costly rite of mummification whereby the body was preserved, and the elaborate and invariably very expensive funeral itself, which I gather might have involved hundreds of participants, of priests, relatives and laymen alike.

The Afterlife was conceived of as a spiritual continuation of life on earth and so a dead man would need, in his tomb, all of those necessities such as clothes and food, and also the luxury items which made his life on earth pleasurable. At the same time, the Egyptians were a realistic people and they had a very human fear of death; its inevitability was always before them and prompted them, when possible, to over provide!

How then did they reconcile the inevitable fact of death with the divinity of their king who, as god, must have been beyond man, above mortal and beyond death? ...The answer was to be found in the myth of the god Osiris, who was believed once to have ruled Egypt as a king.
Apparently he was murdered by his brother Set, who seized the throne and took possession of the power over the people, but was eventually defeated by Osiris's son Horus; he avenged his father and in turn became king of Egypt.

Osiris lived on as lord of the underworld and every king of Egypt therefore, after death, was understood to become Osiris and partake in his kingdom in the hereafter.

The whole body of funerary beliefs were obviously originally devised for the king's spiritual survival after death, and we can assume that he alone would have such expectations. However, as time went on other members of his immediate family, his many children and members of the royal court, would have aspired to similar privileges in the Afterlife.

However, Osiris was also given the title of judge of the dead, and in the tombs of king and commoner alike, the deceased in the presence of a the divine assessors was required to make an account of his life on earth... The virtues which he claimed to possess and the sins which he repudiated, are those acts and sensibilities which were weighed in balance by the divine.
The very first people on the earth who, at the very dawn of time, believed that the acts of sin and the opposite acts of giving charity would be weighed in the Afterlife to give the gods of the underworld the balance of a man's character...

However, this was just the very beginning of a cult ideal that constantly developed as people started to pay for offerings of mummified animals to be dedicated to their gods in exchange for a good harvest, good fortune, or for good health. Over time thousands if not millions of animals and birds were killed and mummified as offerings to appease the gods; however, what sort of god, especially one who was creator or curator of the whole world, would be pleased by the killing of, and the ritual sacrifice of millions of happy, healthy creatures!

Strangely, and somehow in tune with the Egyptians, the ancient South American people, the Mayan people believed that the natural world was infused with a spiritual essence. Many gods and spirits were believed to be manifest in the mountains, the rivers and in the sky, and could be embodied as blood, maize and the much favoured water lily. The Maya had their own Pantheon, or assemblage of deities (divinities, gods, immortals). Also labyrinths, underground caverns— consider king Minos and the city of Petra; these underground places really bother me. (Where are they?)

There has been so much built underground and not just earthworks, burial mounds or left-over gold mines from pre-history; there are also many secret caverns, chambers, catacombs, churches, labyrinths, tunnels and even cities (such as Petra) built long ago deep into the rock of the earth.

But why would any human being build underground when it is so dark, damp, cold and so very unnatural for any human-being?

The *Cambridge Encyclopaedia* has this to say about the City of Petra:

City of Petra; Ancient rock cut city in Maan, governorate, East Bank, south-west Jordan. In *2nd Century AD, a wealthy commercial city for several centuries, controlling the international spice trade; approached only via a series of narrow ravines, included numerous underground temples, tombs, houses, alters and shrines, and a theatre carved out of red sandstone and now a world heritage site.*

The Bible talks about the Father, the Son and the Holy Ghost. So I know of the Father and the Son, but where exactly is the Holy Ghost? Makes you wonder, doesn't it? (Come to think of it, there is an essential difference when it comes to the tomb of an Egyptian king and the tomb of Christ. The former is always found to have a mummified body wrapped in grave clothes, whereas the latter was found to be empty with the grave clothes neatly folded and put aside.)

CHAPTER SEVEN

Actually, I must have been thinking about this the wrong way around...

I mean, feeling embarrassed about remembering past life experience was not my wish, but must have been imprinted onto my conscious mind by interactions with negativity throughout the whole of my own childhood experience, and not because I felt the slightest bit unsure, insecure or crazy. But now after so many years, I have come around to realise that spiritually remembering who you are, who you once were, and where you have been, is evidence that we truly are far more powerful than we are taught...

The human body is a splendid thing, beautiful and engineered down to the very last thread vein; however, all the physical strength and all the natural beauty in the world only amounts to a vehicle without an operator; a machine without a power source. A flesh and blood body, the human form in particular is just a complicated vehicle designed exclusively to maximize motion, strength, purpose, resilience and an incredible sense of sensation. The body was not designed in itself, with longevity in mind—nothing physical can live for ever! Without a spiritual force within, the body would just fall to mush on the floor without any point or purpose and never move itself once.

To my mind, we have not evolved from ape-man or caveman. For thousands of years the ideal view was that God had created us, but the modern view is that we have been genetically engineered to be much better than we should have been and that genetic modification is still working and we are now still evolving! Anyway, who in their right mind would let natural selection decide who lives and who dies when we are actually talking about the children of God or the creation of the gods? I have got it right now: we are the children of the gods and we should be immortal simply as a side effect of having a detachable mind and one day if we learn and grow and have faith, then we will all be able to control our multiple lives and always remember who we are!

From *The Secret History of the World* by Jonathan Black. (Chapter7, page146.)

To modern sensibilities the fact of a story being allegorical (representative) makes it less likely to be an accurate depiction of events. Most modern writers try to drain their texts of spiritual meaning to flatten them out in order to make them more naturalistic (everyday acceptable) or, if you like, only one dimensional!

The people of the ancient world believed that every single thing that happens on earth and in the underworld was guided by the motion of the stars and planets and the mood of the associated gods, so the more the narrative brought out these 'poetic pluralities' the truer and more realistic became the story.

Therefore, to elucidate my point; it may be very tempting to view mythological journeys into the underworld as made by Hercules, Theseus and Orpheus as mere figures of speech, as fantasy (or as a metaphor). ...I believe that it is true that on many levels their writings of adventures between lives actually represent the beginnings of humanity's coming to terms with the actual reality of death and consequent rebirth.

So in trying to imagine these adventures though the underworld by these man-gods, we must not conceive of them as being purely internal, mental experiences or as dreams like we might consider them today.

But more like, when these stories are told to us, or as we read them in Homer's *Iliad* and the *Odyssey*, when these ancient heroes battled with monsters and demons, we should imagine that in the stories being passed down, these man-gods of the ancient world were really believed to have confronted supernatural forces and were backed by spiritual influences which helped them to survive transmigration and return to mortal life.

So we should understand that these stories tell us that they were making spiritual journeys after the mortal death of the body, and fighting monsters in the underworld, that were real to them, in every sense of the word...

However, like many others, I have been re-programmed by my peers, by my education and by today's society to feel ashamed and embarrassed of my belief in spiritual influences, of the immortal soul and of my own memories of past lives. Throughout all of my formative years I learned not to talk about it, covering up the details of them and sometimes trying hard to forget them altogether.

...Whilst at the same time, we are taught about the Father, the Son and the Holy Ghost, and taught about the resurrection of Jesus Christ, and in Heaven and in Hell, all supposed to be historically factual and all spiritual matters that concern the ways of God, the Holy Ghost and the spiritual life of the soul after death. But then the moment you open your own mouth about memories of past life experiences you are obviously insane and a complete embarrassment: but why?

However, all of my memories are intact and at my age now I am eager to reveal all of my secrets. Somewhere along the line I may have been entrusted with some knowledge of past secrets, the old-religion perhaps, yet is still very relevant to our civilization today; who can really say what a human-being is, when we are still developing? Who can say what we will be in the future? Nobody knows how powerful we will be and because of the great outbreak of Philistinism, otherwise known as the reformation, our true destiny is a lot further away than it should have been...

I am not a Philistine (someone not interested in culture), nor a member of the flat-earth society. Instead, I believe in Harmony, in *ying* and *yang*, in matter (something with spatial extension) and in anti-matter (its opposite), a powerful, invisible, ever-present, spiritual, ubiquitous and timeless form.

To my mind, for the spirit to be able to fly through the sky, transmigrate and reincarnate into a new life, this is not a romantic notion or a supernatural fantasy. It happens and it happens quite naturally, and it happens because we live in a great big biosphere full of energy which cannot be depleted or destroyed; the energy you use to be 'you' is a timeless form and will recycle. The big question is, can you control it?

And any subsequent dismay, disbelief or hilarity at the notion by sceptics will have been brought about by a selfishness for some to appear to be brilliantly educated with dogma, people normally perfectly reasoning and accurate in their understanding of the world when actually they have been misled by narrow-mindedness and single-mindedness and their perception of the world is not accurate.

Meanwhile, let us think about the Egyptians' *Book of the Dead*. Apparently much of it is as old as the Egyptian civilization itself and thus creates the question of where the book originated from. Its actual purpose was to be an instruction manual for the transmigration of the Soul. It was an instruction book for the dead, on how to overcome all the dangers in the afterlife and enable the traveller to assume the form of several mythical creatures, and equips him with passwords for admission into the various stages, or levels of the underworld.

See **Fingerprints of the Gods,** by Graham Hancock, published by Mandarin Non-Fiction.

Is it a coincidence then that the people of Ancient Central

America preserved a parallel vision of the perils of the Afterlife? There it was widely believed that the underworld really existed, comprised of nine layers of strata through which the spirit of the dead would journey for four years overcoming the dangers and obstacles in his way (page 154). The different layers of the underworld had very self-explanatory names, like the 'place where the mountains crash together', the 'place where the arrows are fired', the 'mountain of knives', and so on.

In both Ancient Egypt and Ancient America it was believed that the spiritual form of the deceased travelled through the underworld in a boat, accompanied by 'paddler gods' who ferried him from stage to stage. The tomb of 'Double Comb', an eighth-century ruler of the Mayan City of Tikal, was found to contain a representation of this scene. Very similar images were left behind by the Egyptians in the Valley of the Kings of Upper Egypt. The big question then is whether it is just a coincidence that to facilitate the deceased's spiritual journey through the underworld, both early civilizations thought it necessary to be accompanied by a dog-headed deity, a bird-headed deity and an ape-headed deity.

Also, is it a coincidence that one of the stages of the Ancient Egyptian Underworld, called the 'Hall of Judgement', involved an almost identical series of symbols? At this juncture of the spiritual journey the heart of the deceased was weighed against a feather of truth, and if the heart was heavy with guilt it would tip the balance. The god Throth would note the judgement on his palette and the heart would be immediately devoured by a fearsome beast, part crocodile, part hippopotamus, part lion, that was called 'the Eater of the Dead'. (Page 154.)

The Greek Underworld, The kingdom of Hades. From the Book *World Mythologies* by Duncan Baird Publishers.

The underworld is frequently encountered in Greek Mythology, its gates guarded by Cerberus, a monstrous three-headed dog. It was ruled by Hades, the brother of Zeus and Poseidon; however, he was usually excluded from the normal list of Olympians, because his realm was opposed to the celestial Olympus. The underworld was where the souls of the dead mortals were judged and, if necessary, were also punished in the dark infernal regions. However, it also encompassed the lands of the divine dead, the Elysian Fields or Islands of the Blessed. One tradition followed by Homer and placed Hades in the sunless region beyond the great river Ocean which surrounded the earth, but as the Greeks discovered more of the earth a new tradition located it in the very centre of the earth, connected to the land of the living via unfathomed caves and rivers which flowed partly underground such as the Acheron in northern Greece. The Acheron (also known as the River of Woe) was one of the infernal (demonic) rivers. The other rivers connected to the underworld were: the Styx (the River of Hate) which surrounds the underworld, the Lethe (River of Forgetfulness), the Cocytus (River of Wailing) and the Puriphlegethon (River of Fire). Charon, the boatman of the underworld, ferried the souls of the dead across the River Styx and sometimes, in some of the ancient tales, other rivers also...

In Greek mythology the exploits of mighty and fearless individuals are second in importance only to the gods, and people revered these heroes in much the same way as they paid tribute to their ancestors. Indeed, the great heroes were often looked upon as national ancestors, founders of the great families and cities of Greece.

The word 'hero' was used as a term of address by the Princes who inhabit the world of Homer's great epics, the *Odyssey* and the *Iliad*. In these earliest of Greek writings the word means a great person, a prince or a king who often enjoyed a special relationship with the Olympian gods and other deities. Achilles, for example, was said to be the son of Thetis, Sarpedon, the son of Zeus, and Odysseus the favourite of Athene. (Page 147.)

From the Celtic World. Otherworldly Voyages.
World Mythology: The Illustrated Guide, General Editor, Roy Willis. (Page 187.)

The Irish Adventures and Voyages tell of journeys to the Otherworld, a mysterious, ambiguous place. Although its powers can be hostile, it is essentially a place of timeless content, feasting and enchanted music, where old age and death are unknown. It can be entered through caves and lakes, or through chance encounters with its representatives, who invite or entice mortals to one of its dwellings. Its many names include the Plain of Two Mists, the Land of the Young and the Land of the Living. In the Voyages it is often the Promised Land of the West, and located in the ocean or beyond the seas.

In the adventures of Conla, a woman seen only by Conla himself calls him to the Plain of Delight. Conla's father, Conn of the Hundred Battles, orders his druid to prevent the invisible woman, whose voice they could all hear, from luring away his son. The druid's chanting drives her off, but as she disappears she throws Conla an apple. For a whole month this apple sustains him; he refuses all other food or drink, and the apple does not decrease. A great longing comes upon him to see the woman again. When she does appear to him a second time she tells Conla that they can go together in her ship, and he follows her. They sail away never to be seen again...

CHAPTER EIGHT

I have always remembered the difficult life of a Prussian Soldier (1900-1917).

Just how amazing are we really? We don't know where we came from or how we came into being, the missing link still being missing. I doubt very much that we have evolved out of the murky waters of the primeval swamp solely by natural forces and end up as beautiful and as serene as we are. In nature the natural forces of the earth allows for creatures and other animals to evolve into a generic type. By that I mean that all the animals on the earth are very similar, i.e. one lion looks and behaves very much like the next, except in those who have been contaminated by human contact. In the wild one badger looks like and behaves just like the next. And any polar bear looks and behaves just like the next and so on and so on.

Humans do not follow the same guidelines as those laid down in nature for the evolution and survival of the insects and the animals. Why not? To my mind, if there is a God who created mankind, or if we were ever cross-bred or genetically engineered, then the greatest dream for our future must have been for us to be very different from each other, person to person, culture to culture. It must have been desired for us to be very individual, each with an individual personality with individual strengths and creativity. That must be true because we all view the world around us and the events that happen in to us in our lives differently. We are all individuals with our own very specific skills, very diverse from other people. Why? Because if we were all the same, we would all be like sheep in the field, although we would be more like monkeys in the forest, just sitting around only concerned with the local supply of bananas. If we were all the same colour, the same height, with the same attitudes, we would perhaps be happy, but unfortunately we would also be very stupid! Being completely different from each other and even sometimes being very angry, aggressive, arrogant, difficult, selfish, and hateful towards our companions, actually creates the best thinkers, the best problem solvers, the best Diplomats, the best Soldiers, the best Chemists, the best Scientists, the best Fighter Pilots, and it has to be said, the best Astronauts and so on and so on.

...It has to be said that having different opinions and having different desires and goals brings about conflict and conflict promotes thought, and war promotes invention, and those two things combined are the only things needed to drive our race forward towards our perceived destiny!... And that is why we are made to be different because God gave us a destiny! My perception of God or gods will better put me on the map with other great thinkers, such as Aristotle, Descartes, Einstein and Freud.

If the human-race followed the same guidelines as laid down by nature for the entire animal and insect world, we would not have evolved into this particular being, and certainly not into this most beautiful monster... So, somebody, or something, somewhere along the way has given us a hand up, deliberately and wilfully through the creation of this *extremely powerful mind,* whether that be by the hand of the Almighty God, or through genetic intervention, or by some intentional interbreeding with other intelligent-evolved beings from beyond our earthly realms!

For all of time, through all generations of man, we have seen the Masters of our Civilization and of Culture coming through, rising to the top of their industry, i.e. the Artists, Poets, Scribes, Musicians, Singers, Dancers along with the greatest of Craftsmen, Mathematicians and Scientists. Every Art, every academic subject, and every science must have its own Master. The destiny of our Race is engraved very deep into our very own DNA and it's been in there for a very long time, and what is more, Mother Nature did not do it.

There is another side to us, though. I haven't forgotten it— history proves that we can be cruel, very cruel. Along with our abilities to imagine, to create and to perform the beautiful things we have through disputes, conflicts and wars with our own kind, we have developed the Atomic Bomb, Chemical Weapons and many means of torture for our fellow man, leaving us with the grand title of the beautiful-monster...

Mankind has no beginning, no evidence of evolution, and there is no missing link, we just appeared here hundreds of thousands of years ago and very much in the condition we find ourselves in now.

So, created, bred, interbred or genetically modified, we have been made to be the best that could be made. We are most probably the children of the Universe and through mis-management, lies and other arguments, we have lost knowledge of just how powerful we can be!

Spirit guides on the other side or Angels pointing the way?

I was so embarrassed about this part because it sounded more impossible than the rest of my story. I was going to completely omit it, seeing as I have already published it in *The 3 Lives of Peter Miller*. However, spirit guides on the other side have been mentioned by many other Authors, so why shouldn't I tell the whole truth about my story?

I can remember that after I was shot and killed in the War, I lay silent upon the grass as if it was my death bed; after all I should have been really dead, but I remember somehow that I was not! It was my mind that continually lingered on, rather like not being able to go to sleep; in some ways my mind appeared to be tossing and turning, sort of agitated... But so convinced was I that this continuous musing was impossible, I continually tried my hardest to shut down my mind's activities, simply by just ignoring it... You believe exactly what you have been told in your life... But it's simply not true that death is the very end, because it is not; the moment of your death is the very beginnings of your next experience, and your sub-conscious mind knows this!

I cannot say how it is that I recall these things; it's just a gift, my special little talent I suppose, but I still remember all these things today, as clear as a bell. I was shot dead through my left-hand side, through my abdomen, lying down on my right-hand side in the wet grass. I could not move and I was silent but my mind would not shut down so I was just pretending to be dead, telling my mind, begging my mind to 'shut up' or 'shut down'.

I might have achieved some respite for a while because it was not constant, but I remember being very quiet when this person (or thing) started talking to me.

I have no shame in admitting to everyone that I was scared beyond belief. This person that I could not see or touch spoke to me directly, through the mist, just as if he was a man speaking into my left ear and he persisted. And I ignored him, but he still persisted until I somehow engaged in conversation with him or my mind was engaged with it…(him).

So Angels or Spiritual Guides on the other side are there; and the best advice he could give me was to pretend to rattle hazel nuts in a paper bag! No Angels with white feather wings, no trumpets playing a fanfare, and there were no cherubs—just advice on how to rattle a bag full of nuts. Again, I say that this has caused me great embarrassment. Why? Perhaps because I did not understand it.

Today through the intricate detail of my memory alone, I can analyse this activity. You must realise that my body was indeed dead, very dead. I had no arms, no legs and no physical body— that had all gone, disintegrated, disappeared. I could not see the battlefield or hear the sounds of war; all I had was my imagination, my over-active mind and this very strange advice. So it came to the moment when I accepted the advice and pretended to 'rattle my nuts'. So what possible benefit could this strange imagining do for me?

Well, for one thing, if you are given a task of concentrating on such an absurd thing, you stop instructing your mind to shut down; you focus on a problem which proves that you are not dead. Secondly, all your memories are locked up in an energy field that needs to be stirred up, moved around, recycled and thus, re-remembered. All energy of every kind needs to move. So by using your mind, albeit trying to perform a simple mental exercise, and this I believe was the eventual outcome, my mind came back to life, in its entirety. Then, thirdly, by being mentally active, not so much as rattling hazel nuts in a paper bag, but I was charging and discharging all of my sub-atomic particles and becoming alert to the thought of new life-giving opportunities. It is a strange coincidence that I now learn that all types of energy, not only moves, but also rattles.

So now at least I understand that in death, you must not deny your mind's continuing self-awareness and functioning individuality... But that you must use it to find the path in front of you, that perhaps may be through faith, or it might be through self-belief; but in many years to come, if we try this approach to death, then we might eventually find out that this will be an accepted form of science!

So I am saying that the mind continues to exist after death and has an eternal sense of self-awareness. However, if I am right and this is true, then the mind needs a powerful energy source and it needs to be self-contained, after death, within some form of magnetic field! But this is not an impossible dream. Both the invisible timeless power for the mind, and a self-generated magnetic field could indeed exist to protect the mind/soul/ or psyche after death and in-between incarnations!

Understanding the Earth's Mysterious Energies

For some very strange reason, as a child and as a teenager, I was, rather than being interested in ordinary everyday things that generally entertain the young, much more interested in batteries, magnets and magnetic fields. You could, back then, buy a beginner's science set, which including magnet and iron fillings which entertained and intrigued because of the invisible but still very powerful force which attracts the iron fillings to the magnet.

Separated only by a thin piece of paper, the iron fillings instantly follow the shape of the underlying magnetic forces; this was both a powerful experience and perhaps a spiritual one, leading me later on to be fascinated by the earth's own electromagnetic field and other mysterious energies which ebb and flow within the earth and within us, which might also have had some bearing upon my confusion about that **which powers the mind.**

Have you ever had an electric shock from an inanimate object, like metal railings, from a bicycle, from the metal bodywork of your car, from a metal radiator? Anything containing metal that moves along, or around, generates electrical forces, and if you are travelling in it or on it, your body is likely to be electrically charged as well. Then, incidentally wandering down to the local shop, you reach out to grab hold of the handrail and *crack*, an electric spark leaves your hand as it earths out on the handrail.

At my old secondary school it was discovered that if you dragged your feet (in leather-soled shoes) across the fitted floor carpet, in a matter of minutes you could charge yourself up, then touching a metal radiator with your fingers only minutes later would result in a significant electric shock or an electric discharge. Not being a scientist, I am not sure which way round it actually was!

The *Cambridge Encyclopaedia* describes **electrical and magnetic properties of solids:** Electrical and magnetic effects exhibited by matter, because the atoms of which it is composed contain charged components, and the binding forces between the atoms are electrical. Magnetic effects arise because of the motion of electrical charges.

The *Cambridge Encyclopaedia* describes **a magnet** as: A source of magnetic field; always with two poles, named north and south, since no isolated single pole exists; like poles repel, opposite poles attract. A permanent magnet is usually made from ferromagnetic material which at some time has been exposed to a magnetic field.

Magnetism: Described as a phenomena associated with electric fields and magnetic materials. All magnetic effects ultimately stem from moving electrical charges and all materials have magnetic properties. Magnetic poles: The two points on the earth's surface to which the compass points. The north and south magnetic poles have exact geographical co-ordinates and move very slowly with time.

The *Cambridge Encyclopaedia* explains **Magnetosphere:** The region surrounding Solar System bodies having magnetic fields, in which the field is confined under the influence of streaming solar winds. It is a teardrop-shaped region whose size and shape is constantly readjusting to the variations of the solar wind...

At the same time charged particles from both solar wind and the Earth's atmosphere are stored in the terrestrial magnetosphere, which has been extensively explored since Van Allen 'radiation belts' were discovered by Explorer 1, in 1958.

Stored particles are periodically ejected into the North and South regions of the atmosphere along the magnetic field and accelerated to high speed by mechanisms which are as yet 'poorly understood'. Collisions with atmospheric particles cause emissions of light seen as aurora.

Atmospheric physics: The application of physical principals to the layer of gas surrounding planets, especially our own planet. The subject includes such fields as thermodynamics, convection, gas density distribution, condensation, fluid mechanics, radiation and heat transfer. It allows for an understanding of cloud formations, solar heating, the origin of wind patterns and other features essential to understanding the weather and pollution control...

My point being, the earth apparently has a solid inner core, with all the molten lava still flowing around the earth's outer core, and is still constantly burning up and releasing long-lived radioactive isotopes of potassium, thorium and uranium. Then there are the Earth's tectonic plates that constantly push and grate against each other producing other massive amounts of energy. Then there is the rapid spinning motion of the earth with the combined effects of the solar heating of our atmosphere and the effects upon it by the sun, solar winds and solar flares.

So without pretending to be a complete boffin, it is obvious that there is a great deal of electrical-earth-energy being produced which we cannot see or feel with our bodies' normal senses. However, these energy fields are constantly charging, moving, flowing and dissipating between the earth's crust and the atmosphere to maintain some harmony between positive and negative charges.

Currents of electrical force move in and around and through the earth along ley-lines and faults and fissures in the earth's crust, which magnetic fields also flow along, around and through... We should all also know by now that the surface of the Earth, the Earth's crust, is constantly producing or emanating a residual amount of background radioactivity, which is apparently normal, and that is there without the activities of any man-made power stations and other various military forces testing of Nuclear-weapons, underground.

I mention these things only as an observation of the vast amounts of electrical energy running on, in, around and through this Earth. So we must live in a positively **charged electro-magnetic** environment! Even if we cannot see it or feel its effects upon our own bodies, it still must cause some unseen phenomena. However, it is not talked about very much, but your mind does have an electrical element (albeit a microscopical element at a subatomic level).

Your physical body carries energy within itself and your mind has electrical energy within it. This, I am postulating, may be itself contained by its own magnetic or protective force in life and in death. Then, once released from the body by death, the sub-atomic-mind-particles which in life powered the thought-memory and personality, could feasibly not only continue to exist, but travel through the underworld on rivers of magnetic force emanating from, flowing around and flowing through the Earth.

My point being, the **EEG Machine**... In Hospitals they use an Electroencephalograph machine, to measure electrical activity in and around the brain, pinpointing various areas of mental activity whilst the subject performs a variety of different tasks.

And don't allow yourself to think that scientist know all there is to know about the human mind, because they do not; for the most part, the human mind is a mystery. How the mind works in the fashion that it does is one of our biggest perplexities. I doubt if it has been said before, but our minds are not inanimate, our minds are sentient (living self-consciousness). But the mind still needs some kind of power source that is not just bread and water, not flesh and blood. This is an Electro-Dynamic mind that we are talking about here. It has Atoms, Electrons and Protons, Sparks and Quarks (some of the weakly interacting large particles)—in combination, culminating in a swirling hub of a sub-atomic energy where constant thought manifests itself.

It cannot be easily destroyed, it can only be-charged (perhaps by rattling) or dis-charged (perhaps by disinterest and lethargy) and again, if I am anywhere near right about this, then it's pretty obvious to me that our spiritual forms could easily be trapped inside of the body during life, but at the moment of death, could rise up out of a body and still exist...

Obviously I am not pretending to be an academic, nor a **scientist or physicist.** However, the rudimentary science behind out-of-body-experience, life after death and the transmigration of the soul and what ancient thinkers called the underworld has for me at least just become one step closer.

This is about my Wartime Memories... The thing is, memories of horrible things are easier made than memories of good things. Most of my memories of previous lives are about the horrid bits—the loneliness, the hunger, the worthlessness, the cruelty, the head lice, that sort of thing. I have much weaker images of the front and back garden, the noise of my younger siblings and as a child in another country of playing in the street with a ball. So where are all the 'nice' memories? Are good times and good emotions not strong enough to carve out a timeless memory? Are all the good times to be forever lost?

One of the real problems with remembering things is, it is far easier to remember the horrible things that happen to you, rather than the good things that happen to you. It seems that fear is like the point of a knife when it comes to remembering, as it cuts much deeper and this is yet another reason why I really do believe that I have remembered at least two of my previous lives, and my previous deaths. I am not going to repeat my story out of *The 3 Lives of Peter Miller*; however, if you have read my second book, you will know that I remember standing as a child, outside of my home and not wanting to go inside. This must be a very unsettling thing for any child to experience, for whatever reason. I also remember boarding the black carriages of a steam train and heading off towards the war, which, surely, anybody would find rather frightening. Remembering the dirty floor of this carriage, the terrible smell and the often arrogant attitude of the other, first time soldiers must have been part and parcel of a protracted, terrifying experience: leaving behind mothers, fathers and younger siblings on the platform crying and wailing in such pain, likewise constitutes, and becomes, a continuing, terrifying experience.

So where are the *good* memories? There must have been some, but I obviously cannot remember any happiness. Crawling through the muddy trenches and finding it difficult to crawl through mud whilst holding up a heavy rifle and remembering, very clearly, that I really was not looking forward to killing innocent men even though they were called 'the enemy' was clearly an agonising time for my conscious mind and difficult for my sensibilities to accept.

However, perhaps there was one incident that I think I quite enjoyed, and that was being photographed in the trenches by a man with a wide-brimmed felt hat with a camera in a wooden box held up on a wooden tripod. I hope that picture was published in a German Newspaper and that one day, someone will find a copy of that photograph and I hope to be able to identify which one of those young first-time soldiers on the Western Front was me!

Actually, I am not too bothered about my previous lives any more. I believe that I experienced one life at sea after being pressed into the fleet of Portugal. And then in another life I fought as a front line soldier and died again. Remember, I have lived with these memories all of my life—it is not like I have had a sudden revelation. And besides, the journey into my memories becomes even more fascinating when I say to you that I can also remember being Dead!

Searching back through my mind to that very moment of being shot in the back, it was excruciatingly painful and rather distressing as my bowels were trying to escape through the gaping hole in my abdomen where the bullet had passed through me. But even after death my mind continued with its constant narrative. I was thinking, panicking and trying to understand how my mind was able to continue with its abject ramblings even weeks, even months after I had died. And for me even now, included with the memory motion picture of these events, **there are still raw emotions deeply embedded which my mind can also access,** including fear, sadness, pointlessness and confusion. For fifty years I have inadvertently known the fact that we humans have something invisible inside of us that enjoys a 'continuous sense of self-awareness'!

Now, fifty years later, I have discovered that there are other people in this world who also believe that this is an actual fact of human nature...!

CHAPTER NINE

Mankind's natural Psycho-Dynamic-mind...When we are discussing the possibility that our souls (our minds and our personalities) have the ability to continue to be very self-aware of its journey through time after death, then we must conclude that we are made of something else, that is, something other than just the grey fleshy matter that we call brain material which is trapped within the cerebellum.

This other thing must be self-contained within a physical mind in life, and yet still be self-contained after being released from the body by physical death. This other thing must be self-sufficient for power or efficient in harvesting some power from the surrounding electro-magnetism of this world and it would be very small and invisible to the eye.

I would like to say that I have discovered this long lived, life after death ability of the human mind myself, but sadly I have not. This knowledge has been known for a very long time and that is why there is so much written about immortality in mythology.

So we do not just have a physical brain, we have a metaphysical mind, and I wish to call it a *psycho-dynamic-mind*. This refers to the power and the mechanism behind the ability for the personality to survive after physical death and it is self-contained and for me, seems to have the ability to maintain a continuous sense of self-awareness throughout all of time, in life and in death.

This powerful eternal self-awareness has not evolved through time on this planet, and I do not believe that evolution on its own would ever develop such a thing; however, I am thinking that it might have been artificially created long ago by God's own hand, or by some other early technically advanced alien visitors' genetic intervention or experiment.

There are whispers spreading through the dark academic world that suggest that Mankind was genetically modified on purpose to create in mankind a detachable-mind. That is, detachable from 100% of our animal instincts and requirements, and the mind becoming detachable from the animal to enable it time to think also became self-contained and self-sufficient. And by now, for most of us anyway, our minds most probably contain vast quantities of memories of life experience that we could access if only we had the tools! There are reservoirs of many different and varied life experiences to tap into, and it also seems to me now that we have our own unique reservoirs.

However, whilst we are presuming what our spiritual nature is today, we should look back at the past ages to see if there is any possible connection to the knowledge held by our most Ancient of Ancestors. And yes, of course there is a connection, a very distinct and definite connection, seeing as very nearly all of the Ancient Civilizations of our world believed in the abilities of the human spirit to pass through the underworld to live in the next life, and for some, it was also believed to be possible for the spirit to travel across the sky before being born again as a Star!

Now in the 21ˢᵗ Century every schoolboy knows about the Ancient Egyptian civilization; we learn about the extensive burial chambers in the Valley of the Kings, we learn about the great pyramid builders themselves, and we are told about the Book of the Dead. But then we all, very promptly and politely, forget all about them, and why? Because what they were building, why they were building, and what they believed in just seems too difficult for us to understand, being even too weird for most of us even to contemplate... However, at some stage, we must look back and see exactly what it was that they were doing!

A piece slightly adapted by myself from *THE MUMMY*, by E.A. Wallis Budge... Concerning Mummification. (From page 173 of the above-named book.)

Mummification ...The practice of preserving a dead body with oils, herbs and spices, for an indefinite period of time. A mummy being the universal word for this practice and, literally means, the mother of the undying soul (i.e., to preserve the body indefinitely keeps the spirit awake).

The word *Mummy* being the term given to the body of a human being, male or female, adult or child, animal, or a bird; Lion, Cat, Cow or Bull, even a reptile would have been mummified. In fact the Egyptians mummified the bodies of everything they could get their hands on.

....The body of which would have been prepared by removing anything which might immediately spoil, all of the internal organs, the heart and the brain material removed most often by a metal hook worked through the nasal passage, and all that remained was the physical carcase of the person which was then preserved by means of bitumen, spices, gums, and/or natron.

...And as far as anyone has so far discovered, the word *Mummy* is neither a corruption of an ancient Egyptian word for preserved body, nor of the more modern Coptic form of the hieroglyphic name. In other words, *Mummy* was not in any way a term given to mean 'a prepared body' or 'a preserved body' or 'a mummified body', but was simply meant as 'the Mother'.

The monuments discovered, both above and below ground, (adapted from the Preface of above book) and the many remains and artefacts of ancient Egypt preserved in the great museums of Europe and Egypt are chiefly of a sepulchral (burial or tomb) character, and we owe most of all their great and often ingenious constructions entirely to the belief of the Egyptians that the soul would never perish, but that at some unknown point in the future, the soul/psyche/mind would someday return and revivify (animate) the mummified body. But why would they think such a thing?

These people were actually very clever indeed; they were neither savages nor infidels; they had a very great understanding of a very great many subjects, including agriculture and astronomy, so why would they be so stupid as to think that the spirit could come back into their preserved body, now with no internal organs, no diaphragm, no lungs, no heart and no brain material left intact and magically re-animate this body, live in this body and be physically alive again? No.

It must clearly be a misunderstanding or a mistranslation. These early Egyptians surely must have believed that the spirit would live on, as long as the body remained preserved on the earth, in the earth and not decay (not ever putrefy).

And this is most surely borne out by the considerable care, consequent on this belief, with which they embalmed the bodies of the dead, so that they might easily resist the action of decay, and be ready for the return of the soul was without question, immense. Even after the embalming, the preservation of the embalmed body, in tombs, catacombs, caves, and in burial mounds, was the chief end and rightful aim of every Egyptian who wished for everlasting life.

However, as I have already said, I truly believe that their imagining returning into their own embalmed body is a popular misconstruction of the fragments of evidence that was left behind. In my heart, in my mind and in even deep in my soul, I understand that nearly all of the Ancient Civilizations of our world knew very well that the inner spiritual form would be knocked out of the body upon death, and even more so, upon a terrifying or violent death! Their understanding and their meaning must have been far more precise, in that it was the wrapped up preserved body that literally was the 'mother' of an immortal soul, coincident on the fact that the body would now last forever and the spirit would have to roam.

...Removing the brain matter and the internal organs as part of the mummification process intentionally gives access for the internal application of preservatives which keeps the body intact and imperishable. All this in the belief that the soul, at this stage, still separated from the body, survived, but after the mummifying process, would not return to the body, but rather, could not re-enter the body (there being no place for it) then to rest! Thinking instead that when the originating body was protected from decomposing, then the spirit would be free to roam the earth for eternity!

But no, you will say that is not the full story. They must have believed that the spirit of the dead would try to re-enter the preserved body at a later date because of the vast amount of burial goods interred with the wrapped, embalmed, preserved body within the Tombs, often things such as their Horses, Chariots, stored vases of food, weapons, armour, golden jewellery and for some, even their servants and soldiers!

...However, and again I even think that this is a misconception, because as I have previously mentioned, everything that exists in life constructed out of matter also survives on the other side as structures of pure energy—ghosts, if you like.

They had buried with them enough food, earthly goods, weapons and transportation to provide the necessities of life, but in the other world/ on the other side. The fact is that when you are dead and gone, you have not died as such, only moved over into a mirror-like world where everything still exists, every house, every church, every cathedral, every road and every horse and chariot!

The practice of mummification was practised by many of our earliest civilizations, not just the Egyptians. I believe it common knowledge that the Sumerian people, the Inca and the Aztecs practised this art as well as the Celts a little closer to home.

The Egyptian 'Book of the Dead' existed to continue that line of understanding down through the ages and through the generations and it contained ritualized instructions for the writing and drawing of magic tokens, spells and incantations specifically to aid the spirit of the dead to successfully pass over.

In particular, I have noticed their very frequent use of the picture of a white bird, in full flight, with a human face, on many of their funerary items!

...Perhaps no civilization has been quite so occupied with it, or put in so much of the very great attention to detail, not in the vastly elaborate and ritualized ways of the late Egyptians. Nevertheless, trying to preserve the bodies of the dead and bury them along with some of their weapons, and with some of their precious items often of gold, silver, jewellery and decorative garments of armour, with the obvious intention of freeing the spirit to live immortal lives in the Afterlife whilst the originating corpse lay wrapped in linen (or in other geographical locations compressed into a sack), to be preserved for all of time, was all over the Ancient World, a very common practise indeed.

CHAPTER TEN

Where do Spiritual people come from?[1]

In around 5057 BC in the region of Mesopotamia, now known as Iraq, the birth of a great leader was foretold. We should imagine his mother as being no better than a peasant woman, perhaps living in a small mud brick hovel in a small agricultural community. The story tells that it was in the depths of a cold winter when food was in short supply that a plague struck. Tongues were wagging in the community, accusing the young woman of bringing disaster to the community through witchcraft.

Then, in the fifth month of her pregnancy, she had a nightmare. She saw an immense cloud, and from it emerged dragons, wolves and snakes that tried to tear her child from her body. But as the monsters approached, the child spoke from inside her womb to comfort her, and, as his voice died away, she imagined (saw) seeing a pyramid of blue light descending down from the stars. Down through this pyramid of blue light came a boy holding a staff in his left hand and a paper scroll in his right. This boy's eyes shone with an inner fire and his name was to be Zarathustra...

This child grew to be the boy his mother had dreamt off, but the forces of evil knew their greatest enemy had come down to earth, and they were just biding their time.[2]

It is said that Zarathustra had a mission of his own, a set destiny to spread the Zoroastrian tradition and lead his own followers against a whole host of spirits and demons, and these form the basis of today's classifications of demons and spirits that secret societies still believe in.

I have included (and adapted) this very short part of the tale of Zarathustra because it seems important to impress the fact that many people from all around our world always have and many still do believe in monsters, demons and in spirits coming down to live on the earth...

As I previously wrote in *The 3 Lives of Peter Miller*, my own spiritual journey took me from being a living, breathing teenager serving as a front line Prussian soldier, to lying in the grass beside the trenches being very quickly dead!

Perhaps because I was still so young, my mind was very reluctant to dissipate, and lingered on. This lingering on turned into restlessness and confusion when a long time had passed and my mind was still conscious of itself and rigorously refused to be quiet!

Back then I recall that, apart from my own thoughts, I was only aware, externally, of being completely surrounded by some kind of hanging (suspended) electrical (sparkling like stars do at night) mist, my mind at the time struggling to come to terms with this strange phenomenon of eternal awareness, as when you want to sleep but your mind will not be quiet.

Obviously, as I have said, I remember lying there dead and yet pondering on the subject of time because it (time) was still there. I knew that obviously: however, although it had no real bearing upon me anymore, it still existed for everybody else!

Then I was spoken to, or should I say that I have always believed that I was interfered with by the spirit of a man, and somehow given advice on how to pretend to rattle imaginary hazel nuts in a paper bag!

Any person could go mad thinking about the absurdity of such a memory and perhaps one should keep it to himself. But I have spent a very long time thinking about these memories and now it appears to me that after death, the conscious immortal mind struggles to adapt to a different world, without being able to rely on the eyes, or on the body, which naturally provided sensations of touch, smell and hearing to create a mental picture of what is real and what is going on.

The mind must accept death of the body and adapt quickly, then at least attempt to conjure up some images to explain what it is somehow still aware of...

There is no distinction between night and day when you are dead. There is no feelings of cold, hot or hungry; on the other side there is just your mind in a whirl, grappling with doubts within this 'hanging' electric mist.

It is only afterwards in life again that you can try to unravel this mystery. Understanding time on the other side is really hard; probably because it is no longer necessary, you are hard pushed to tell if you have been dead for nine hours, nine days or for nine months, and it seems to me now that I was dead for forty-four years—that being the time between 1917 and when I was born to this life in 1961...

Anyway, going back to the spiritual memory of being given new life, I remember a force of desire that was definitely not of my making. It was desiring of my presence, and then I remember being drawn up through creaking doors and into a spiritual temple with a round roof that appeared to be something like the Pantheon of the Gods which existed in Athens.

Again, I wrote all that I remembered word for word in *The 3 Lives of Peter Miller*, and my perception was, and still is that this place was circular in construction with a very round or high vaulted roof. I remember it being similar to a very large spiritual temple, where the gods stand in wait for you all around the perimeter, set back, almost hidden in dark alcoves. My memory makes this quite clear that among the many other figures, I stood in front of a solid stone carving of Zeus, seemingly carved out of white Marble; it was he who gave me choice of a new life from the book. Whilst I was being bathed in blue starlight which seemed to twist its way down into me, long lines of information apparently concerning different lives appeared right in front of me and then just as quickly disappeared from the pages of this book!

... Also, just as I previously wrote in *The 3 Lives of Peter Miller*, I was somehow given the choice of a new life based on the information given to me. I had to choose between sex, health, ambition and intelligence! However, after accepting a new life; after accepting this new life, I was pushed out by other strange but powerful forces... I literally fell through the floor as it was disappearing from under my feet and after flying over land and sea, then travelling through a dark tunnel, I was born again!...

These ancient gods who reside in the alcoves of this round temple seemed to know me from before and they had a very great amount of influence over my physical being and also, it seems, over my destiny.

I used to think that this magical place must be where my true beginnings were... and on death my immortal spirit must somehow have migrated back there to the Pantheon of the Gods in Rome. Or was it back to the Illussia Mystery School where I might have started out (thousands of years ago), as an initiate of spiritual learning...?

In life most of us have sight, sound, smell and touch sensations, which help us to understand the world we live in. I am saying obviously that when you are dead and your soul is set free, that it is very difficult to gather information about what is happening to you without the benefit of any such physical sensations. But that does not mean you're completely dead.

The mind, the soul, or the psyche, whichever name you prefer to call it, does live on, continually, in exactly the same way as it feels during an out-of-body-experience.

...For the mind there is eternal conscious awareness, and what the mind cannot see with mortal eyes it still tries to remember, describing its surroundings as white electric fields and ebbs and flows of energy and the mind tries to remember this as a series of picture images.

If I lived in Greece long ago, and if my suggestion of/or hypothesis on mummified bodies literally being the mother of an immortal soul, and if my original life was back in ancient Greece and my original Greek body might have been mummified way back, then and in subsequent deaths my spirit might wish to migrate back to its cultural homeland after being released by the death of the mortal flesh.

I am not so arrogant as to expect very many people to believe this; however, I remember after being shot and killed in the trenches of the Western Front of 1917. My spirit lay undisturbed by any mortal hands, but it lay instead in a kind of turmoil, not actually being able to rest, more like a troubled night's sleep filled with anxiety until being awakened and instructed by my spirit guide. Yes, we conversed—I have admitted as much already, but apart from one thing, I could not say what we conversed about!

The only advice he gave me that I can remember was strange indeed; it was for me, that is, it was for my soul to imagine rattling nuts in a paper bag. Why this was his best advice I will never know, but imagine rattling hazel nuts in a paper bag I did. Was this activity suggested just to keep my mind active? Was it some kind of test of ability, or in the spirit world after death, can the Gods hear you making such a sound?

His advice worked well enough. At some time after rattling and rustling my imaginary bag of nuts, a door became visible to me as the white mist cleared before me. It seems that the Gods can hear you if you make enough noise. These doors were huge in comparison to my tiny being. In many ways I could describe the size of these heavenly doors as not needing to open at all, because I felt that I could have squeezed through the keyhole or even slipped underneath, but, the heavenly doors that I remember opened nonetheless.

Apart from the white mist that surrounded me and the huge wooden doors opening, there was nothing else there. There were no angels, no cherubs, nothing with wings and there was no fanfare. If I ever intended to write an imaginary tale, don't you think that I would have included some of these things?

I remember being drawn inside by a powerful force. This is not the same feeling as of being pushed, or moving under one's own volition. I say it exactly as I remember it. I was being drawn through these doors as if by a magic force and it was only once inside of the actual building that I felt that I could move on my own.

Now my arms and legs appeared to be formed from the wind and by the dust of the ground and I now walked over slabs of grey and green. The paving slabs beneath my feet had veins of red and blue running right through them. The roof above my head was domed, rather like a vaulted roof with one perfect circle, right at the apex, where a twisting shaft of starlight shone down upon my spirit, and it was the only source of light; all around me there was darkness and the statues of the Ancient

Gods lurked hidden away in the alcoves, six on one side and six on the other, twelve in all and all equally spaced apart.

They—these ancient gods I presume—detected my presence and one apparently even knew my name. "This is Prometheus, he was once one of us... The fallen one... He now lives the life of a mortal."

I remember being embarrassed because I could not remember the names of my gods even though in my previous lifetimes I had had enough opportunity to learn their names and to worship them. Was that the feeling of some guilt or inferiority?

The book of life lay open before me, held up high on an Alter where I was able to, even required to, read the lines of words that were now appearing across the top of the page in front of me. Seemingly, these lines of words were descriptions of lives that could be lived. Three different lives were presented to me on the pages of the Book of Life. The first life was that of a boy who digs for Diamonds, but his life is short and rather unhappy. The second life that appears on the page, and directly underneath of the first life, is the life of a woman, who, herself in life gives birth to four children and she is happy.

For one reason or another I dismiss these two lives and rapidly moved my gaze to the third line which was being revealed to me; it is a man's life of intense uncertainty and with periods of great confusion: often falling in love, this man has love affairs with beautiful women which ultimately end suddenly but this never quells his lust for life...

The father of two beautiful children, he becomes a successful writer of Philosophy and the bringer of joy to many… And after reading these details, this was the life that I chose for myself…

In death I eventually rose up into heaven and entered through its doors, yet I did not remember any Angels, no Cherubs, there was no fanfare, no music of any kind. Although I have always regarded this place as being something like Heaven, it lacked much in the way of splendour and spiritual opulence that one might have expected. My memories of this event still seem too mechanical and far too orderly to have been heavenly and yet this was how I remember being given a new mortal life by my marble gods!

CHAPTER ELEVEN

What can possibly power the human mind and the immortal Soul?

Being driven only by a curiosity to explain how I have past life memories, I can only focus on searching for the truth about the hidden mechanisms behind the ability of the human mind to experience continuous self-awareness, through life and through death. As I keep on saying, I am completely convinced that I have remembered my former lives, and very well remembered (through sound, through smells and through moving images) being conceived, as you will see in chapter thirteen, growing in the womb and being born and that convinces me to postulate (presuppose) a theory.

I believe that we human beings all have detachable minds! (Detachable from the physical needs and the daily demands of the body.) And even more startling, I think that in the ultimate death of the body, the mind completely detaches from the body as its normal physical magnetic restraint collapses.

This, as I choose to call it, psycho-dynamic-memory-mind, or the soul, is powered by an inherent electrical and invisible force which in life is protected by an electro-magnetic force provided by the physical body. I suppose that if you had the type of machine that could register this protective force, it would most probably appear as a brightly coloured Aura or Halo, encircling and pulsating all around your head... An interesting idea or what!

The universe rattles with energy; our world by its very nature is an enormous electric generator spinning in space; a consequence of the generation of electricity is the manifestation of the earth's electro-magnetic field, which saves us all from charged solar particles entering our atmosphere and from solar flares.

The *Cambridge Encyclopaedia* describes the **Earth's Geomagnetic Field** like this: The magnetic field of the Earth which arises from the metallic core, and which may be regarded as produced by magnetic dipole (transmitting aerial) pointing towards the geomagnetic North and South poles. The positions of the Poles have varied considerably during geological time, and can be studied by analysing the direction of residual magnetism present in rocks and iron ore.

We are living out our lives on the spinning surface of an electric generator and living within a beneficial and protective electro-magnetic field. All of our physical movements are activated by electrical charges and our thought processes and the desire to do something/anything all arise from a spark of electrical charge conducted by the synapse.

Synapse = connection between two nerve cells. The specialized junction between two nerve neurons, present in the nervous system of all animals. Nerve impulses at the axon terminals of one neurone are transmitted across the junction either chemically (by neurotransmitters) or electrically (by local currents) to influence the excitability of the other neurone...

The Mind is an entity also called the soul which originally was supposed to differentiate between animate and inanimate nature. Aristotle thought that plants and animals all had souls. Later philosophers ascribed the mind only to people, supposing it to be the one thing that unifies our experiences, makes our experiences our own, makes self-consciousness possible, initiates our actions and desires, and makes possible our continued identity through time. Descartes claimed that an immaterial mind is what makes freedom and immortality possible.

It seems that we (humans, animals and plants) are not just made up of a combination of different materials forming an evolved structure of matter and size (mass), but that we are all a combination of the visible matter (minerals, proteins and salts) and an invisible and as yet undetectable force of flowing electrical currents and electrical fields which we use to motivate both our thoughts and our actions. When the body mass experiences a great physical trauma or indeed in the inevitable death of the body, the invisible matter which is our very own electrical essence (at sub-atomic level contained in a mass of electrons) that can leave the body, temporarily, or more permanently. At the moment of our death, this electrical essence containing your feelings, emotions, memories of experience and your personality could (with the will-power or the desire to do so) continue to exist indefinably in the ethereal world, free of body but still confined within the magnetic field surrounding the Earth.

Seeing as there is some disparity between people's understanding of the mind, soul and thought processes, I am going to call it the **psycho-dynamic memory,** to describe the possibility of our invisible and electro-dependant personality of existing intact for all time in a continuous stream of self-awareness and of being able to reincarnate.

This is not a belief in anything supernatural but a belief in something that is meant to be a very natural part of our human psychology. There are obviously many different types of power in this world that we know about and there may be many more types of energy that we will discover over time.

But for now we do know that there is electrical energy, both flowing and static, and there are magnetic fields which surround the earth and surrounds us and protect us.

The earth's geomagnetic field protects the earth from solar flares and solar winds, and I think that there is enough evidence to suggest that our soul, the psyche and the mind, call it what you will, could use some of this invisible, timeless energy to continue functioning without a physical host.

What force is behind the creation of the Universe and inspires life to exist everywhere?

CHAPTER TWELVE

In this life I love Psychology and I love Philosophy. I love philosophy because at its very roots, it questions whether this world is just material, or spiritual, or both! Philosophy literally means the love of wisdom. In general, the intention of philosophy is to deal with some of the most difficult questions about our universe, this world and mankind's place in it.

Is the universe entirely physical in its composition and in its mechanisms? Is this world perhaps a metaphysical paradox? Is there any purpose to it? Can we know anything for certain? Are we really free to make our own choices? Are there any absolute values that we can rely on that will not change over time?

Philosophy differs from science, in that the questions cannot be answered empirically (by trial and error) by science or by experiment or by religion. Its principle is entirely intellectual, and allows no role for faith or revelation. Philosophy tends to proceed by an informal but rigorous process of conceptual analysis and intellectual arguments. Philosophers also have to question the nature of their own enterprise; i.e. what philosophy is, or what it should be in the future, and how it should help mankind—questions that in themselves are philosophical questions.

So what are we then? Mortal, just flesh and blood without a sparking plug? Are we spiritual, and just assume that we have some amount of physical solidity, or are we a combination of these two types of things = some sort of Psycho-Dynamic-Electric-Man?

Looking at an excerpt from **Mummies, Myth and Magic in Ancient Egypt,** *by Christine El Mahdy, published in 1989 (page 11):*

'We think of ourselves as divided into two parts, body and soul, but the Ancient Egyptians in their exquisite wisdom developed a different and far more complicated explanation for the nature of their existence. According to their beliefs, the survival of the body through embalming was necessary for the survival of the other aspects of their spiritual being; the **ka,** the **ba** and the **akh.**'

The infant, it was believed, was placed into its mother's womb after being created on a potter's wheel by the ram-headed god Khnum. But as Khnum formed the body he also fashioned a spiritual copy, resembling the outer body in every way, with all of its needs, its secrets, its desires and expectations. This copy was called the *ka*, ghostly in appearance and stored away deep in the heart. Some of the great kings of Egypt thought themselves as having more than one *ka*, Hatshepsut, a powerful female Pharaoh of the Eighteenth Dynasty, claimed to have nine.

...After death, the *ka* was forcibly separated from the body. Forcibly? (How was that done then, by the preparation for embalming? Is that why they removed all traces of bodily organs and the brain tissue?) The *ka* would then have to inhabit the tomb in a constant effort to be close to the physical, material body in which it had spent its life. And since the *ka* needed everything that the person needed during life—food, olive oil, clothing, perfume and shade from the hot sun , these items were so provided as burial gifts placed in the tomb primarily to satisfy the ghostly *ka*'s continuing needs.

The *ka* was distinguished from the dead person by being depicted in drawings with a pair of upraised arms on its head; or, in **Ptolemaic** times (Claudius Ptolemaeus, 2-C-AD), by the pair of arms itself, shown to have grown legs and arms and carrying a feather fan behind a picture of the actual person.

The *ka* could also be freed from the body during life when a person was asleep or in a coma...
 (This belief being remarkably similar to our understanding of the out-of-body experience.)

The *ba* was not a physical element either, but like the body it was unique to each person (similar to our understanding of the psyche, the soul or the inherent spiritual self). It is perhaps best described as all the non-physical aspects that constitute an individual, what we might today call a person's individual character or their intimate personality. The *ba* was pictured as a human headed bird. (Which could fly away?)

...It was thought to have entered the body at birth, together with the breath of life; and both, left the body upon the death.

Magical spells were said over the (prepared dead body) mummy, to transform it into a form of entity that enabled the dead person to exist in the after-world. This entity, called the *akh*, was believed to inhabit the world of the after-life...

Looking at how I perceive this world, I actually have my own hypothesis of how the mind and our spiritual forms operate; I believe that we exist both in the physical world and the spiritual world at the very same time.

For me, in this life, your spiritual inner being is your character, your intimate personality wrapped up in the desire to evolve, and yet it is trapped (some say buried) within a physical carbon unit, within this body that needs the energy—the Egyptian **ba**. Life must surely be a joint effort ruled by both the physical needs and mortal suffering, (hunger, desire, lust, and probably some ill health and disappointment) until the death of the body whereby the **ba-**spirit is again released.

Now I am saying that the spirit then makes its magical journey around the world or through the underworld, carried along perhaps over time in a full circle by the governing laws of the Earth's slow moving magnetic field. During this time the spiritual form must continue to be aware of its own being; remember that it continually has consciousness and it is also part of my belief that at times you must battle hard to remember this before reincarnation can take place.

Strong belief in cultural religion might help you to return to your original homeland and faith in your cultural gods may also be beneficial. Communication between spirits seems to be possible; however, self-belief and faith are required, lest you forget. If you forget your faith, and deny yourself perpetual awareness, perhaps you can drift off into a spiritual coma where you literally forget who you are!

Our world is divisible into two separate but incredibly interwoven and inter-penetrating powers or mechanisms. The visible: the solid world built out of Atoms and electrons, dark matter, molten metals and the minerals on which we believe that we live, stand and sit on. There are also the invisible forces, which, according to some, constitute the power of God, the Holy Spirit or, from my point of view, the all-powerful but invisible highly charged field of electro-magnetism which science calls our world's geomagnetic force which protects us, and our atmosphere from solar winds and flares of radiation from the sun!

Our geomagnetic field is, in every sense of the word, exactly the opposite of the solid stuff we choose to call matter.

You cannot see it, feel it, smell it, or touch it, and yet it must be here, right above our heads and right beneath our feet!

It would seem that facts of common everyday knowledge are apt to lose their significance through too great a familiarity. Like stars in the night sky or the powerful currents of the oceans, in this way, through complacency, people have forgotten that they are there.

Another fact of this character is that when a baby is born it must awaken into life; something other than the smell of the air and wet grass must activate this young creature. I was born in the country and my very first job was on a mixed farm and I worked with many farm animals and have been lucky to have witnessed many births. Often it is not immediately apparent if the new-born calf, lamb or goat is alive or not, until it stretches out with its limbs and draws in its first breath.

Witnessing such a thing brings about the thought that the material substance composing the body of any mammal, any baby boy or girl, or any such baby creature is merely the means of expression of a life, through some motivation the vehicle for pleasure seeking and universal purpose, a conductor for use by other invisible forces which at times, as in still birth, are not there—just like material substance in a condition called inanimate is often a conductor for another force called electricity, which does not exhibit any willing, personality or consciousness of its own.

If you destroy the human body there is no manifestation of its life force; the ghost does not remain: destroy the wire and there is no manifestation of electric light as the bulb grows dark. And in much the same way the human body appears to be incidental to the individual spirit of consciousness, awareness and personality, as a wire seems incidental to the production of electric light.

For me, conscious thought and indeed subconscious thought, has to be reliant upon some electrical energy making connections with stored memories of previous movements, emotions, situations and experience as a background light for the manifestation of our thought process. That said, one would really expect to find some sort of filing cabinet within the brain tissue for storing masses of experiences, and also you would expect to find some sort of battery within the body which supplies this much needed energy; however, there are no such things!

The body of any living being must have some amount of free-flowing life force provided for it by the immediate environment and the ordinary world around us, which is, by its very nature, full of invisible energy. (Or we will have to thank God for sharing the Holy Ghost.) To my mind even the slightest movement needs some electrical impulse; however, having seen babies born, and in my life I have witnessed human babies, lambs, calves and baby rabbits appear at birth, I know that sometimes there is no immediately visible signs of life. Sometimes not immediately in those few seconds after birth, until the new-born being moves for the first time or is provoked into movement by the manhandling of the mother—when it is motivated by desire and, using its own inner power to move muscle, opens eyes and takes that first breath. It is that invisible and undetectable force from within which animates and motivates the body into life and there is no evidence in the world that anyone can show me that will prove that this inner spark of energy has to be brand new!

Every part of my body is made up of a multitude of substances that have been here on this earth for a very long time. There is no part of me, at sub-atomic level, that has come from outer space; all of my physical self has been recycled. In much the same way as I turn on the cold water tap and fill a glass with water to drink, there is a very great possibility that this cold water has been drunk before. Water is water, millions, if not billions of years old. Just because it has been cleaned and comes straight out of my tap, this does not mean that it is brand new! The power that provides for the thought process and memory connections in my head maybe, by the same token, recycled...

As children, many it seems make accidental references to previous experiences that they could not possibly know from their youthful activities or from their surroundings or from their new uneventful little lives. I have witnessed such accidental references to very unusual previous experiences from all of my children before they were even of primary school age and just once, from my stepson, when he was around nine years old.

As adults we have developed enough self-awareness to understand our personal presence, understand what the real world around us is, and we are supposed to have enough confidence to relate our individual experiences to others. We become confident enough to tell the truth!

This is why so many people relate their experience of, and express their deep concerns after having an 'out of the body experiences'. A human being is a self-analysing, self-aware, recorder of time and events and if we have any doubts about our perceptions of experience, then don't we shut up for fear of humiliation and embarrassment?! Every person's account of continuous stream of awareness of his or her own existence outside-of-the-body should be taken very seriously indeed. The evidence mounts.

What if the Ancient Egyptians were right? For the most part of the Egyptian Civilization the people believed that after the death of the mortal body the spirit was released from its bonds and would be able to roam the world as an immortal soul. There is no way on earth that these people expected a soul to return into the embalmed corpse as this practise was to create an immortal soul, not to re-animate the old dead body.

Ultimately, I have to agree with some parts of the Egyptian analysis of what makes up the psyche, and also agree with Sigmund Freud's uniquely similar description of the mind, in the suggestion that the mind has three separate parts in so far as the *id,* the *ego* and the *super-ego* co-exist. The *id,* being short for identity. These three parts of the mind might also reflect the changes in man's thinking due to his maturing years, the *id* being the originating identity, the *ego* being the child, and the *super-ego* being the adult version.

However personally I believe in a fourth stage of our spirit; that would have to be the *rise* (the rise of the repressed *id* spirit from within).

I am saying that the immortal soul, which is reincarnated at birth, is the *id* part of the mind which was with you at the moment of your conception. However, although the *id* is the very oldest part of you, over the years of your life it has to be repressed by the *ego* in childhood, and also again repressed by the *super-ego* in adulthood. Both the *ego* and the *super-ego* are far more connected to the physical and solid side of this life in, i.e., desire, lust, greed, family, education, career, power and success paths, all associated with mortal living.

Ultimately I suggest the *rise* of the repressed *id* spirit from within, or, to put it another way, the *rise* of the residual or resident identity emerging now with some very strong influence for the first time into the conscious mind as the desire of the *ego* and the *super ego* weaken with age: this rising of this part of your mind, the real self, it could be argued, might be the most probable cause of what we call mid-life crisis, where persons around the age of fifty – fifty-five years, often wish to go on exotic trekking holidays in the Himalayas, buy powerful motorbikes, get divorced and then remarry and also often develop a great desire to write and publish books... it's probably the rise of the repressed spirit!

The single purpose of my explaining to you about the soul and my trying to postulate on how you can have your own timeless yet individual spiritual form, is, I believe, exactly the same today as it would have been in the Ancient World—to prepare you in advance for your inevitable journey through the Spirit world and to help you develop spiritual strength through knowledge and understanding of a very unique possibility; and preparation is self-belief and begins with Faith.

In this world, so full of static electric energy, flowing electrical and magnetic forces, lightning bolts and solar winds playing against our atmosphere, we would be really stupid to think of our minds purely as material flesh and blood, buttons, push rods and revolving gears. No Way.

There is far more to the activities of, and the form and function of the mind, than we have ever been told. Obviously, we do know that our every breath, our every mental thought, our every memory and our every physical movement, is initially instigated/and motivated by an electric charge occurring somewhere from a synaptic nerve ending down through a nerve and then jumping across another synaptic nerve ending where its message is understood. So even in the most basic of examples, our minds do use some small amount of this natural electrical energy to remember, to think and to function. This natural energy within us does not always need a body, but makes use of one time and time again and may very well be a timeless form...

...This is not really turning out to be very much like the poet's romantic or the idealist view of spiritual reincarnation. The distance in time between lives is indeterminable. Where you end up seems to be uncontrollable as is the amount of clear memory of your former self which you are left with. However, as we find our spiritual 'feet' we might one day learn how to speed up the reincarnation process, and learn how to efficiently navigate through the underworld: and if we work at the faith needed to be able to remember these supernatural facts of life-in-death, then our minds may become stronger and more able to remember who we are and what we are, to a much greater extent...

At least the concept or the idea of having an immortal soul or an eternal awareness of experience, might be a little bit closer now to being explained and I can explain why I remember previous lives and remember being dead!

To sun up: The three overlapping dimensions of your mind are the *id*, the *ego* and the *super ego*. The *id* is the immortal soul, the *ego* is the child's mind, and the *super-ego* is the adult mind.

CHAPTER THIRTEEN

I say that I can remember my past lives, and I remember being shot dead, and I say that I can remember the experience of being dead, which is very much like not sleeping very well and your mind tossing and turning and going off in tangents all night without finding any real peace.

Some would say that I am living proof that we, our souls, have a continuous stream of awareness.

However, remembering fragments of past lives is just one piece of the cake that is easy enough to swallow. Having a continuous awareness means that after death your soul travels over land or through the earth, with no eyes or ears, no sensory organs of any description and your soul has to interpret what is happening by intelligence or by attachment to some memory of previous experiences.

In this life I have had great problems in understanding the conception memory, and had thought for many years that I had actually flown up to the doors of Heaven and on into some Pantheon of the gods where I was allowed to gaze upon the words revealed in the Book of Life.

However, one day, not so long ago, whilst I was musing over my memories of the Book of Life, I realised the truth of the matter actually lies in the very structured order of these remembered events. I had overlooked this for years, but now it is abundantly clear to me. At the end of my soldiering days I was shot in the lower back and killed. I lay in the grass both dying and then dead, but confused as my mind continued with its conscious awareness. I was literally 'plagued' by my mind's own determination to expect more of life, and not to let go of its consciousness. I was literally experiencing denial of death!

I have been an idiot for all of these years, but then it is not as though you can ask anybody else to explain the unexplainable. Yet the truth was always staring at me right in the face. At the end of my previous spiritual memories, I was born again into new life, pushed out from a dark tunnel (as I wrote in *The 3 Lives*). I never covered it up; luckily for me now, I wrote about it exactly as I had remembered it, and being born again was the end of my reincarnation process, not the beginning of the process...

Rewinding my mind again and going back to a time from before I was born once again, something had given me a message. I had thought that it was a verbal message; however, I did not have ears to hear it. So it could have been a spiritual message or, more importantly, it could have been a bio-chemical message...

At least I wrote my memories down and published them exactly as I recall them, even though I could not understand them before now.

The truth is all in the actual order of events; if we have immortal souls and a continuous sense of awareness, then after death, what exactly is going to happen? You won't be able to see anything, and you won't be able to hear anything, other than electrical vibrations and the sounds of chemical combinations; this I interpreted as a white mist, surrounding me and obscuring everything else.

...I felt movement, I believed it to be in an upwards direction, but there is no reason why it was not a slow forward movement, as I was carried along as I now believe not by supernatural powers, but by the earth's own magnetic field. Somehow and somewhere, your soul is going to migrate into a woman's ovaries. That is a fact of life: how else are you ever going to be born again?

Obviously the mind is a powerful thing, and it is true that my mind might have created its own construct (memory of some fantastic delusion) to explain what it could not ever understand or to give my life a purpose.

However, I now believe that my mind did not manufacture such a fabulous construct to explain the unexplainable, but instead my mind had memorised exactly an interpretation of what it thought was happening to it, going on around it, event after the event, as it was reincarnating back into physical life inside of my mother's ovaries and then growing inside of her womb!

Being physically born again was always part of this memory, so to explain what really happened one only needs to reverse the order of events, from my actual birth backwards.

…This is my memory of the soul: my soul patiently waiting for something to happen… (From page 23 of *The 3 Lives of Peter Miller*)… "I could have been lying there in the long grass of that battlefield still, with not very many passing clusters of static electric memories (spiritual forms) to communicate with; but I can, in this life, pass on his words to thousands, with the aid of my laptop computer, (and my publisher), just as long as I can remember precisely what happened to me."

…This is a bio-chemical instruction whereby the female egg is constructed around my soul or where my soul enters the egg which sets off a bio-chemical reaction and absorbs all the details of genetic memory… "The spirit calling itself Michael Faraday on the other side had given me the details of his life's work in a conversation we shared (in the spirit world). He had told me in his own opinion the whole truth; '…to want another human life is the key to the door and how to open it,' but before that could happen, I had to find the door which was more difficult because it was (the door) hidden away in another secret place deep within the mist of time" (I thought it to be in the spirit world).

…"You cannot walk there with no legs and no feet, and you cannot fly there with no wings, it is far more a matter of rattling your static electricity, like imagining you're making as much noise as you can with a (an imaginary) brown paper bag full of hazel nuts. Yes, it's difficult but possible. Imagining rattling a **brown paper bag full of nuts** is much easier than finding a hidden door when you are dead, believe me (trust me). And so in-between worlds, I practised all that my spiritual guide, Michael (Faraday) had told me and steadily, over time, I did get better and better at it until the time came when the noise I was making with my rattling seemed to have attracted their attention."

What possible madness could have caused me to believe something as daft as this, unless it was really my memory of the rattle-like frequency of the growth of ovum in the ovaries!

Obviously, if reincarnation is entirely natural, after your death, your spirit must attach itself either to a young male or a young female. I had to decide which case applied to me, although I doubt that it would make any particular difference, so for the purpose of writing I chose to believe that my spirit somehow became attached to my mother, and I again developed within one (or more) of her embryonic cells (eggs)!

...I say that because if I had become two babies (two fertilized eggs), then I rather gather that my spiritual self would have been split into two parts and I would have become one of two identical twins: and that in itself might well be a very controversial thought...

I wrote that... "They beckoned me towards the door which had been there all of this time, but it must have been hidden from me the whole time by the white mist that surrounded me."

...Is this my passing within an ovum, from ovary to fallopian tube?... "Seemingly made of solid planks of very old Oak, the door rises up high above me like the doors of a Great Medieval Castle, supported by many wrought iron hinges set into solid stone walls on either side. I was beckoned towards this great opening, not by people or by other things of life and death, but by some form of desire or the wish of some other, older, wiser intelligence…"

…"As I crossed through time itself, the huge doors opened inwards. Dry hinges creaked as though in desperate need of some lamp oil, and as I passed through the door into the realms of this spiritual temple, the doors closed back (behind me) into its keeps." This was my mind's own interpretation of entering the womb.

I wrote in *The 3 Lives of Peter Miller*… "This is a place that opens desire in your mind, and desiring (a new) life, I now appeared to have new legs and new feet made out of the wind and the dust, and so I walked across a floor that was appearing right in front of me as I imagined myself going forwards. Now I see there are walls of solid stone of grey and green; the stone slabs beneath my feet are tinged with thin veins of red and blue, very well worn by the movement of frequently returning human souls."

Is this a memory of arrival into the womb?… "There is a round roof above, (the roundness of the womb) with a round hole right in the middle at the top where the bright blue starlight streams through in a twisting shaft of spiritual illumination and natural earthly energy, **(the umbilical cord)**, which was shining down brightly, deliberately on to the Alter which holds open the Book of Life…"

… "Now as I approach, I can 'see' the enormity of this very

Ancient place, the alcoves cut back deep into the walls where the marble statues of the wise beings stand and stare, (the gods), each one somehow probing and absorbing all the contents of my mind, weighing up my many faults and vetting my future worth (to the world below)."

…"Six marble statues on one side and six on the other, (these gods, all twelve of them represent the signs of the Zodiac, which also can influence my physical and mental attributes. They are all equally spaced apart and then another bigger, taller statue appeared in front of the Book of Life."

...Now I wonder, who was he standing in the very centre of this place with a long carved beard behind the Alter...

(Could this memory have been, either my own interpretation of God, who was in the act of giving me this new life opportunity, or as I now prefer to think, that this big, powerful man of character was my mind's perception of what was being created? Or looking at this moment in time physiologically, could this large white shape actually have been the physical connection that I shared with my mother? The very shape of the connection between embryonic sack and the wall of the womb before it becomes an umbilical cord.

… "It is warm and moist here (but not damp), although there seems to be no air or wind, so far as I could tell. I sense the curiosity aroused in the gods which surrounded me, and hot breath on the back of my neck **(very first physical sensation felt by the developing foetus)**, as one speaks out after sensing my presence within the walls of this Ancient Temple of Wisdom."

I wrote... "This creature was once one of us," he said loudly without ever moving his stony, cold lips... (I would have remembered his lips as unmoving because I could not see him, or them. It appears to me now that I was remembering my mother's biological reaction to falling pregnant and accepting the condition.) "This creature, once one of us, could easily become one of us... *is now*, one of us!..."

..."This creature is the fallen one, his name is Prometheus." (This part could well have been a passing memory of my former lifetime and my name in Prussian might have sounded something like Prometheus, or else it could have been a desire on my mother's part to have a boy child.) "...and now he suffers life as an immortal... and he could be very useful to us, if he would only choose a new life and stay strong. Thus the voice proffered to his Ancient and stony faced friends"... (or this could have been the now developing physical form of the foetus recognising the *id,* the reincarnating soul who really does bear that name!)

.... "Now they know who I am; they also know that I have come again into being; now they have my number and they can feel the weight of my consciousness holding me down. I instinctively know that they all know of my story like the backs of their hands. Then right in front of my very being the pages of the book are flipped over as if a magic wind had blown them over to a specific page—although I can easily see that the pages of the book are motionless and carved out of solid stone!"

... "My inquisitive mind now desires to know more and I am beckoned by the bearded one to look upon this new page;

there are words writing themselves and it becomes clear for me to read as a list of three lives…"

(Could this really be a memory of receiving complex streams of DEOXYRIBONUCLEIC ACID (DNA) and choosing, or was this reviewing my intricate physical characteristics?) Remembering a list of three lives is mystifying in itself; looking back upon these memories now I think what a specific number of lives revealed to me, i.e. in conception there are three people coming together to create a new person: genetic material from my mother, from my father and the spirit of my previous self = 3 lives….

…"On the first line is written the intimate details of the life of a woman who has four children and she loves her four children and she is happy." (I obviously did not want to become a woman.)

…"The second life that starts to appear beneath the first, is of a boy who has to dig for diamonds. And he is treated very badly and painfully dies; although it sounds awful, there are benefits to be had from owning this boy's short life." (Perhaps I perceived this set line up of chromosomes that were revealing themselves as chemical combinations and instructions that contained some illness or some disfigurement which badly affects the longevity of this new person. The phrase 'digging for diamonds' might actually suggest a perception of someone short in stature or someone desperately greedy.)

… "As it appears to me in my mind, this young boy dies at a time when a great opportunity is available to him to be somebody again, and I am really interested in him—but why?" (Perhaps our lives have crossed before, or was this possibly some emotional response or empathy?)

… "But then, as I read on the words start to disappear because if I do not accept this boy's life then I cannot know what great things are in store for him later on! It seems that each life is connected in all fairness to equal measures of happiness and suffering, yet one often precedes the other unless you perfect your understanding and choose very wisely." **(This I believe to mean that you cannot have everything perfect. Is there a natural balance, can you have an intellectual mind, a fantastic memory, be seriously strong and be very healthy: The question is, is perfection even possible?)**

… "The third line reveals itself and it is a man's life of intense insecurity and periods of great confusion; often falling in love, this man has love affairs with beautiful women, affairs that ultimately end suddenly, but this never quells his lust for life." (Perhaps the chromosomes lined up in this order implied a healthy and lustful physical life combined with some ambition for learning.)

… "The father of two beautiful children, he becomes a successful writer of philosophy and the bringer of joy to many. But, just as soon as I have read the details of this life the words start disappearing again and (subconsciously) I have accepted this life." **(As I have become a writer and published Author, I naturally must assume that I accepted this combination of physical and mental attributes.)**

... "And I am being drawn out of this place..."

... "It is not my will to leave however, far more that I need to know before I want to go back, but they won't let me know any more than what I have already read." **(The egg is fertilized and the new DNA strands are now complete.)**

... "In my first mortal life I never was taught to write and in my second mortal life I was only able to pen but a few words, like my name and my address; never had I before this imagined being an author or imagined ever being the bringer of joy to many!" (If this was revealing an ambition to write, then it must have something to do with the wishes of my *id,* **spirit.**)

..."I tried hard to hang on to those words, struggling to remember them, even though something was trying to delete that memory. Some strange and unimaginable power was reaching inside of my mind erasing that which I had only just learned from the pages of the Book of Life!"

Here I was always convinced that I must have been losing something which was well beyond my reach of understanding, and probably would have been beyond anyone's comprehension. Obviously, being in the womb is rather like being inside of a temple, it is a warm, comfortable and relatively safe place to be. However, when the warm womb waters (the amniotic fluid) break, a completely natural event, the foetus will probably react with some degree of alarm.

I am convinced that here my mind actually registered this event as actually having had something removed, which had actually only recently been given, i.e., the warm amniotic fluid.

... "But I used every ounce of my desire to grasp that content of my mind, somehow immediately making exact copies of memories of that event and then making even more copies of memories and so on and so forth, much to the annoyance of my peers..."

THIS IS THE VERY, VERY IMPORTANT BIT....

I said in *The 3 Lives* that I made copies of memories and then made even more copies of memories and so on a so forth; well, isn't that statement too close to actually describing the event of multiple cell division to be ignored, more cell division and more cell division ad infinitum, which is exactly how we develop from embryonic sack into a baby and then into a child?

It was not memories that were being taken from me by the gods, but rather my warm surroundings were diminishing; however, I must have interpreted this event as a great loss of personal-mind-space, which in itself raises new questions about what contains the mind in life?

Back then, in a probable and understandable panic, I must have assumed that the space my mind occupied was being removed and that I had attempted to copy all of my memories to protect them from immediate danger and retreated into the physical mind of the baby, and this is perhaps the very reason that I believe that I can remember my conception, my time in the womb and subsequent birth so vividly.

..."Why would anyone or anything give you beneficial knowledge and then take it back again almost immediately, especially the knowledge that I need to fulfil my chosen task? But I fought with them there, using every ounce of my desire just like Michael (Faraday) had told me to, with magic and spells, but it had cost me dearly..." **(As I have previously said, but it is worth saying again, perhaps in the womb your mind not only occupies the brain material but also occupies the surrounding amniotic fluid.)**

..."The system that was had taken random chunks of my conscious mind, knowingly taking from me some of my energy and it seems that I have forgotten some of what I once knew very well. I know that I have made the gods very cross with me." (Page 26 of *The 3 Lives of Peter Miller*.)

... "A powerful wish on others' behalf forces my departure, (birth contractions) and I am being pushed out by powerful convulsions, like a baby is pushed from the womb; the floor of the temple evaporates from beneath me and the walls seem to melt back into the mist almost before I have exited through the floor of this once protective space." (My words, "the floor evaporating" now sounds amazingly similar to a baby turning in the womb ready for birth and the seemingly unusual movement of the surrounding walls and floor of the womb. I thought for many years that this was all in the clouds above the ground.)

However, it is obvious to me now, that exactly what I have remembered for all of these years is the imagery (the perception of events recorded as memory in pictures, to describe physiological events) my mind used to record my conception, my development in the womb, my surroundings within my mother and finally my rebirth!

I also wrote… "Now land and sea spread out beneath me. Flying something like a bird on the wind, I am heading down and along to the West, bits of me **(my subconscious I guess)** somehow having a proper destination and I am flying over land and sea that I recognise from an old mariner's map of the oceans that I have seen before with my real eyes."

… "The land and the seas have more colour in them now than I remembered from the map and then I believed that I must have missed my proper destination, passing now over the edge of what was known to me and forcing me over lands that are new to me, and I remember feeling lost." The womb probably being quite light, do I remember entering the dark as my head engaged in the vaginal tract possibly?

… "Now my passage is quickening and I am afraid of crashing into the earth and rocks and naturally fear the worst possible end to my unplanned spiritual journey…" (A difficult birth, maybe leading to fearful thoughts or empathy with my mother's anguish?)

… "But then the most amazing thing happened to me. I was blinded by the light at the end of a long dark tunnel and I am able to draw in my first breath of air."

… "My arms and legs felt like warm marshmallows. I felt rather intoxicated perhaps (cumbersome and ungraceful) and my speech when I tried to talk was a ridiculous wail. I wanted to immediately stand up on my new limbs but I was unable to as I was suddenly wrapped rather tightly in a towel and laid in my new-mother's arms."

... "It sounds ungrateful to complain, but I had expected more, much more and faster..." (End of Quote.)

I have to repeat that the basis of my story is my exact memories of these strange events, and that they were first written and self-published by myself seventeen years ago, in a collection of papers called *Manmade God*; these were written and published exactly as I have always remembered them from my very birth.

For many years I thought that between lives I really experienced a spiritual journey back to my original homeland, to the Pantheon of all Gods in Athens, or a return to my mummified body hidden somewhere in the ground and such a belief was not easy to talk about. However it was not a spiritual journey.

It was my mind, not imagining an artificial construct to give my life purpose, but was my mind trying to understand, and remember what it was experiencing. Or, put more accurately, it was the original, *id* part of my mind; the *id* being short for original identity, recording the events of my spirit moving into my new mother's energy cycles and memories of the events of becoming an ovum (the message by my spirit guide?). Memories of receiving lines of coded chromosomes from the DNA of my mother and from my father combined with the actual thoughts of my inner being.

The choices I must have made were selected from: male, female, strength, intelligence, health, memory and longevity, and possible choices regarding my own destiny (the three lives in the Book of Life).

These were all the memories of the egg being fertilized, my growing movements, physical developments and the chemical changes operating around my foetus, connecting and affecting my very soul...

To summarise: I believe that I memorised all that happened to me simply because my soul was reincarnating and already had a very strong presence of mind, knowledge of life and a continuous sense of self-awareness even before my new body was fully developed and pushed from the womb by the very natural force of contractions. As I wrote in *The 3 Lives of Peter Miller*, I also remember very easily the dark tunnel between the womb (which was light) and the outside world where I immediately wanted to stand up, but could not because my arms and legs seemed to be made of Marshmallow...

I say that I can easily remember the dark tunnel between the womb and the outside world, but not quite: to make that statement as accurate as I possibly can, it was rather the blinding daylight exactly at the moment of birth that I remember so well...

THIS IS WHAT IT REALLY FEELS LIKE TO BE BORN AGAIN...

CHAPTER FOURTEEN

Considering that we are just one Race of beings, living on just one lonely planet on the very furthermost edge of the universe, we seem to know very little about how we have come to be. One would have thought that, like any undisturbed Dynasty (long family line), very accurate records would have been kept about our lineage since the first moment that a writing system was invented. One would have thought our predecessors would have been proud to write about the family tree and the deeds of our forefathers, and who married who, but this is simply not the case... One might also think, that being all of the same race, that being human beings, that we would be a lot more forgiving and understanding of our neighbours and of other cultures in different countries around the world. But that is not true either; all of the early writings seem to be confused about our origins, and report that our race was almost continually at war with each other. Almost all these early records were mythical in nature, and often spoke of spiritual realms and cities of the Dead.

Very early writings from all around the world including the ancient Greeks, Egyptians, Incas and the Maya, have spoken out from the greatest depths of history, of Gods and Angels coming down from the sky, creating the race of Mankind. Sons of God even mating with our women (that is, cross-breading) and they even wrote about some people cheating death by actually becoming immortal and living for thousands of years!

The question is, these early civilizations were not born out of magical fairy tales; they did not evolve through pure chance and were not governed by stupid people with no intelligence: rather on the contrary, the knowledge our early ancestors amassed thousands of years ago was equal to our own knowledge in several well-known fields.

These very early people managed to organise society into a particular order of rank and file with very clearly defined rules which benefited society as a whole, rather than just the ruling families. They developed a system of law and order which was enforced, built ocean-going vessels and traded goods between countries. They very quickly discovered mining for ore and produced a great variety of gold and silver items. All over the world primitive man learned how to farm on industrial scales, do things with complex constructions in stone, made magnificent carvings of their gods often out of solid lumps of granite. Particularly in Egypt, such carvings were produced on a monumental scale. Ancient man also had a very great understanding of astronomy, in tracking the stars and identifying constellations, and I am talking about people who existed on Earth more than four thousand years ago.

...So, if they were so clever in so many such subjects, why would they allow themselves to be fooled by a belief that the inner spirit lives on, first in the spirit world, and then in some afterlife?

Did the ancient people of this earth really understand our spirituality better than we do today?

Have we forgotten what we are? Have we forgotten how powerful we can be? To me, it seems very obvious that we should open our eyes and our minds to what the ancient people of our Earth had to say, and what they were saying was, "We are more than just flesh and blood, in death we can fly!"

...Then if we can listen to them, perhaps we can move on from thinking that we are just some sort of accidental, inconsequential, overdeveloped, needy and greedy, flesh and blood Neanderthal. Then we might be able to understand that we are a combination of very complex flowing energy fields, electrical forces and dark-matter, which in combination makes the mind/psyche possible. And this mind seems to be contained in life by the magnetic forces of the body and yet must still be self-contained after death.

I doubt very much that we managed to climb out of the primeval swamp and learn to walk on two legs, develop communities, develop agricultural systems, start trading with each other and then one day decide to hurt, hate and kill each and every other race of mankind, then forget to write about it! But instead they wrote about gods in the sky, they wrote about Angels and Demons and about the seven layers of the underworld and the afterlife instead. No, I think that we must have had some help at some point in Ancient history and it is the exact details of that 'help' which has been lost forever.

However, there is a very similar story which has been handed down through the ages, and it tells us that our world was made by God, we were made by the hands of God, we are his children, made in his image, and if we believe in him and repent of our sins, our lives will be made over again. (Interesting or what?)

We use some electrical energy every day to motivate the pumping of our hearts, to operate the complexities of our inner organs and the muscular structure, the outer garment of our physical body to explore the physical world, to grow, to learn, to play and to work...We also use electrical activity within our brain matter to make connections between memories and our desires and our necessities. The combination of these three things is cognitive experience; this is a fact proven every day by the use of ECG and EEG machines. (Brain-scanners and electrocardiograph machines.)

That means this power manifests itself not only within the brain matter, but also around the scalp as an aura of energy; it is this energy which powers your thinking mind and your individual soul. There has to also be a separate yet entwined magnetic field which protects your mind, your personality and your identity in life, in out-of-body-experiences and through death to rebirth!

...In the process of out-of-body experiences, and similarly in reincarnation, your true essence, your soul, that is the pure energy that your mind uses to think, function, ponder, reason, remember and desire, and whilst it is being **protected** by its own magnetic field, can exist outside of the body for a very long time, perhaps even eternally without being dissipated.

My own out of the body experience taught me very well, that thinking and reasoning, being self-aware, and even being very anxious about your future whilst being out of the body, is a completely natural event until it finds its way back into the body.

At this time I also came to believe that it is possible that a set destiny can be achieved through a reincarnated life, hence the continued birth of the enlightened ones! (Those who have lived before and now seek understanding and self-development.) However, saying that some people have set destinies implies an ordered mechanism of gifts and an opportunity which is somehow laid out in front of the chosen few, which sounds rather supernatural, but then perhaps it is not so complicated.

We are not actors playing out our parts on a stage; this life we lead is not a game, so any such set destiny, or a personally desired goal, must somehow come from within.

I have already said that a human being comes together through three separate dimensions, or it might be easier to say that a human being exists with three predominant principles entwined. Some people believe that we are re-born, we redevelop and re-educate through the karmic forces. Karmic forces must be very tightly entwined with the spiritual evolution of all of mankind because it can be seen in everybody rather than the chosen few...

Yes, I do believe that an intricate and deliberate mechanism exists to provide a pathway for our spiritual evolution and this could easily have been a deliberately genetically engineered part of human kind!

The first principle (the body) is simply the principle of your own physical being, your new body; physically it is a combination of your new parents' and your grandparents' chemical DNA strands, complete with its faults and slight imperfections and traces of their genetic memory; so physically you will be very much like a mixture of both of your parents but your mind will always be your own...

...However, some people believe that because of karmic influences, your true nature/essence is born under conditions which will provide all the opportunities for the learning of and for the development of the strengths and characteristics you are in most need of. In so many ways it is like letting you be re-born at the bottom of a ladder that, in your new life, you *should* try to climb regardless of your circumstances!

These conditions seem to guarantee opportunities throughout life for increasing your progression and development; in other words, the forces of karma provide the stimulus for your evolution. The framework for this change and growth is set through your exact date of birth (astrologically and terrestrially) and often include other environmental factors that could influence in your growth.

These environmental factors will include your race, religion, close family, your work ethic and culture.

The second principle is free will (the desires of the mind). We all have the freedom to make choices for ourselves and make actions and efforts in those things that we choose to do for ourselves or for others. We are not in any way bound to succeed—indeed, failure is in itself an important lesson for someone who is going to live forever; but try we must, and try our very best to master something, because that is the direction and the attitude that you have to take on.

It is true that once we have been born then many factors of your life cannot be changed. As children we cannot change the situation we were born into; often we cannot even understand it. However, as soon as we become adults, many difficult points of our existence can be manipulated or changed completely just by one's choice of attitude alone.

The third principle is Karma (or is that the desire for opportunity?). Within this principle operates what has been described by some as the Law of Compensation or the Law of Equilibrium. How hard you have tried to progress and how you have used your free will and your free choices in the past is all remembered within one's own chemical make-up as a list of checks and balances. Some people say that this helps the gods of karmic forces to influence the conditions of your new life.

However, I would rather say, that the term *karmic forces* refers solely to the coming together of the surviving spirit with a brand new physical body, which it inhabits, and which jointly provides new opportunities for learning and new activity, or to continue with one's own previous ambition.

Being aware that you are someone who has experienced life before would naturally encourage the desire to further evolve into someone with a better faith, and a better understanding of life, given the opportunity to do so.

However, perhaps it is not quite as simple as that; careful thought and planning of a desired route in which to evolve will end in nothing without foresight, effort and the willpower to succeed, and these three things you have to develop yourself in life through the physical world...

Karma is the **Sanskrit word** which means "To do, or, to make happen". Perhaps it is the energy we use in our thoughts, deeds and actions which requires some justification, for obviously good karma is not just thrown at everyone. Everything we do, everything we try to do, or everything that we make happen provides an opportunity for personal growth, better understanding and better mental development. We should not look at Karma as a mechanism just for debt or credit management of good and bad thoughts, but in providing future opportunities where necessary for personal growth and advancement. Although this may sound supernatural, it probably comes from within and it is not for just one man or one family alone to evolve; but it is for everybody, everywhere!

I wrote many times that I stood before the Book of Life and chose a new path from its pages (by choosing combinations of strengths and weaknesses) where, although some of the difficulties were shown to me, I nevertheless chose the life which was one of the choices offered me, providing an opportunity for learning and personal spiritual growth. (*The 3 Lives of Peter Miller*, page 41.)

It appears that when we make the right decisions and take the right actions, positive and rewarding opportunities open their doors to us. However, these are not doors that can be opened in any way other than by positive deeds, and/or by positive thoughts. To give one reason alone, if you have no interest in development, then you would not be able to recognise a window of opportunity. If we take no pride in ourselves, if we believe mankind's existence is pointless, if we make no effort for positive thought and we make no effort to evolve, then these doors or windows of opportunity will remain hidden from us for all time!

...It seems to me that we are somehow required or hardwired in our genealogy to be responsible for our own learning and for our own achievements; it is not enough just to be here waiting, hovering on the edge of belief, but to desire some purposeful evolving of the mind and consequently the strengthening of the spirit that will follow.

And where, you may ask, is this mechanism that requires this evolution of the spirit? And in answer I would have to suggest that it is hardwired into our very own DNA. Our evolution was never meant to be physiological; the form we have is the strongest and most useful form that we can possibly have, if you only knew it, the most versatile, the most mobile and probably even the most pleasurable form we could ever have.

No, I am positive that we have been programmed to evolve mentally and spiritually to meet our future destiny. It is God's will, if you like, that we should become more like him, and this is etched very deeply inside of our genetic code and belongs to everyone, to every race and creed of mankind.

That said, we must hope that our choices come out a particular and favourable way; but if we are to be truly responsible, we must be willing to take the consequences, good, bad or indifferent, knowing that we should still learn from them. Perhaps it is not unusual to blame everything that goes wrong on society in general, or on other people or on bad Karma; however, bad Karma is the result of bad decisions or doubt or indifference, so being responsible for one's own actions without habitually blaming other people is the key to the lock that we must use.

Where am I today? Well, if I am exactly right in my own thinking, then we do have a spiritual soul and it needs a source of power of some kind, way, way separate from physical needs of, and the daily brain functions of the manipulatable human body. There is energy of some form or another in everything on the earth, in every creature, flower, tree, every blade of grass, in every brick and in every block, so we must have an energy which flows through us and around us, which also powers the mind!

This power of the mind I believe is electric in nature and self-contained, so after the death of the body it is able to escape death, it rises out of the body intact by means of some kind of sub-atomic-magnetic-cage. (In many ways I think it appropriate and important to say it must be similar to Faraday's cage.[3])

This energy is the *id* or later in life the *super-id*; it is you, your mind, your memories and your personality, and it continues to function, aware of itself (as you are in life) and it remains aware of the world's environment through which it must obviously pass.

...So, I believe that we, on this Earth, have at some time in the past, and quite possibly many thousands of years ago, been visited by another intelligent and very technologically advanced peoples, and that we have been, quite deliberately, created, crossbred, interbred or in some way genetically modified deliberately to produce a far different mind than what nature intended for us.

Things that are done which require a very great technical knowledge are seldom done for no good reason.

If we were created, interfered with or crossbred by alien visitors, then there must have been very good reason for doing so. And I am thinking that this must have been done so that we are **no longer completely 100%** earth animal in our nature, and this is borne out in our difference from any other Earthly creature in the way we communicate, in the ways we think about ourselves, in the ways we can be philosophical and in the way we believe that there really is something called God.

The result of this crossbreeding or genetic modification is that we each have a mind that is very deliberately independent, often selfish but individual and **detachable. That is to say, detachable from** the day-to-day needs of the physiological body, allowing our thoughts to focus on other things, i.e., initially to work as miners and traders of metal ores, as slaves perhaps, then later as craftsmen, as soldiers, sailors, scientists, teachers, and so on.

I also believe that as an accidental side effect of this cross breeding or of our genetic mutation, we human-beings now have a mind that is not only detachable from the direct and immediate needs of the physical being, but that it can be detached completely from the physical body through the trauma of a serious accident, resulting in an out-of-body experience and detachable from the body completely in death.

In this life I fell off of a ladder on to a tarmac road, and as my body hit the tarmac, my mind recorded this event not as hitting a hard surface but somewhat like falling onto a trampoline from the same height. Initially, I remember my thinking mind went through the tarmac road and into the earth, just as you would sink into a trampoline, before being, literally, shot up about thirty feet into the air, and seemed to attach itself to the roof of the building where my mind stayed for some time.

To connect that experience with my memory from my previous lifetime, when dying on the front line, my memory and mind stayed inside the body for a long time. Was this perhaps because I was in a state of denial? At that time I remember trying hard to refuse to accept that I had an on-going conscious awareness. Was that the power of disbelief that kept my on-going mind inside a dead body?

... However, I am convinced that normally on the death of the mortal body, the soul is released completely and yet surprisingly intact, into the atmosphere where it will have to travel around or through the earth, being bound by the laws of the earth's own magnetic forces, which, it may surprise you to learn, does not move very fast.

...The soul being, as I do believe, both self-powered and self-contained, as I said, by sub-atomic-electro-dynamic-forces, the journey around the world or through the world between living experiences could easily be remembered as a spiritual journey through the dark passageways of the underworld, as the Egyptian mythology reveals, before being reborn as another physical being!

If this is true then obviously the time and place of death is significant when contemplating the distance and direction of the spiritual journey that the *id* has to take, before there will be any chance of a rebirth, and that statement elicits the need for other new questions.

If I am right about these things and the soul after the death of the body is only moved by the magnetic force of the earth, then depending on the direction of the flow of the earth's magnetic field, one could plot a route that the spirit would take. This anticipates another interesting question: could the people of our ancient civilizations have positioned their graveyards and their sacred burial grounds in an exact position, so that the spirits of those departed might well be re-born right back into the heart of their own community?

I believe that it could be that hundreds of years ago, or thousands of years ago, my body was mummified and my soul continued on its journey because it could not return into its original body to die. If that is true, then there are hundreds of thousands of mummified bodies left over from the ancient past and so I would have to assume that there are literally hundreds of thousands of immortal souls living on earth.

However, that is just one theory of the possible mechanics of reincarnation offered by the Ancient civilizations of our world. I am sure that previously being mummified has very little to do with it because I am actually convinced that it is just human nature to have an independently self-aware spirit which has the ability to return to the flesh again and again for eternity.

I want to come back again after this life, if only to prove my theories to be right and in death I must remember that my mind is still active and not suffer denial again. But perhaps you do not want an immortal life... I am thinking that if you do not know anything about your spiritual form, and if you even deny it, and if you do not believe in and have no faith in any so-called 'gods', then perhaps it is possible for the spirit to stay with the rotting corpse and dissipate and dissolve into the earth after death. A profound—and disturbing thought.

However, and this is where your God comes into his own, this is where your chosen religion (preferred belief system) is very important. If you are interested in coming back to life again after your next death, then it is very important to understand that it is possible to do this: believe that natural systems are in place to accommodate it, believe that the energy which is needed to make this possible does exist, and believe that your immortal soul has a sense of continuous awareness.

I thought for many years that my spiritual journey had taken me back to some place in Athens, and/or right inside the heart of the Pantheon of all Gods, as written in *The 3 Lives of Peter Miller* where I gazed upon the Book of Life. For many of my years I have been wrestling with the concept of one god or multiple gods who have great influence over your life because of these complicated memories of mine. I wondered if perhaps at one time I had been an Ancient Greek or, even better, an Athenian! I also considered whether, perhaps, I was at one time an initiate of the **Eleusis Mystery** school and that with snake pits and drugs in the dark they scared me out of my skin, deliberately to teach me about the reality of the spirit world before killing me and mummifying my body before a ritualistic burial in some sacred site!

We still know so little of our beginnings on this planet; we do not know exactly what we are made of, or what we are really capable of, or what evolution will eventually do to us. I thought that perhaps we have been engineered like the Salmon who have to swim halfway around the world to return to our own original spawning ground. If so, our souls after death would have to migrate to its actual place of birth. The actual place of our spiritual birth is right where your mummified body lies, so maybe I do have a mummified mummy in Athens!

However, as it turns out, I am convinced now that my memories are of something of a more physical nature. My memories of the spiritual temple was far more likely to be where my reincarnating soul was trying hard to understand the chemical changes and the natural mechanisms of travelling slowly along the lines of the Earth's geomagnetic field, into my new mother and of my conception in the womb and actual physical rebirth.

My great temple of all gods was in fact my mother's womb, and the light that shone down through the single hole in the vaulted roof was the earth energy flowing to my new physical being via my umbilical cord. My mind was already functioning because of the existence of my immortal soul, the *id* being present.

My memories of flying over land and sea was an interpretation of what it must feel like for a baby to turn within the womb ready for birth, and my remembered fear of crash landing was most probably from my experience of a difficult birth or empathy for my mother who must have been rather anxious...

If it is all true, then it is a fantastic story, and I believe that I am the first person ever in our history to honestly write about what it actually feels like to be shot dead one minute and remember what it feels like to be 'dead' and remember the exact moment of reincarnating in to new life.

Although it seemed quite quickly, it actually took more like forty four years in time from being killed on the front line to being born again, and if my spirit was travelling directly North from the position of the corpse as I believe it was, then it covered perhaps not much more than ninety to one hundred miles, that is, from the front line of the First World War, where I died in France, to Hawkhurst in Kent, where I was born into this life—in England.

This ability of the soul to reincarnate is not achieved through smoke and mirrors. It is my considered opinion that the soul can jump from one life into the next without any magic potions, and without any magic spells. However, to really experience your next reincarnation, you must learn, and understand, that there really is an earthly and very natural geomagnetic mechanism that allows for your psycho-dynamic-mind, not only to survive death intact, but that also allows your spirit to travel towards a new life. And this is what the Ancient Civilizations taught to the children of the chosen few in their mystery schools. It is a kind of magic, yes, but for me, **reincarnation just doesn't happen fast enough to be of any real use.** Let's face it, to be of any real advantage it must happen a whole lot faster than this and we must be able to remember far more of our previous experience...!

Final thoughts:

Without belief in God you become an orphan.
Without belief in your spirituality you will not remember being born again.
Well, where is the harm in trying to make the most of it? You just don't know who you will be next.

SUGGESTED FURTHER READING

JOURNEY OF SOULS: Case Studies of Life between Lives.
By MICHAEL NEWTON, PhD. Published 29 November
1994

*HUMAN IMMORTALITY AND THE REDEMPTION OF
DEATH.*
By SIMON TUGWELL. Published by D.L.T. London.

HOW TO UNCOVER YOUR PAST LIVES.
By Ted Andrews. Published by Llewellyn Publications, USA.

MINDS AND BODIES.
By Robert Wilkinson. Published by The Open University
Press.

MUMMIES, MYTH AND MAGIC in Ancient Egypt.
By Christine El Mahdy. Published by Thames and Hudson.

OLD SOULS: Scientific Search for Proof of Past Lives.
By Tom Shroder. Published 25th August 2001.

THE CURSE OF THE PHARAOHS.
By Phipipp Vandenberg. Published by Hodder and
Stoughton. London & Sydney.

THE MUMMY.
By E.A. WALLIS BUDGE. Collier Macmillan Publishing.
London.

THE UNDISCOVERED MIND.
By JOHN HORGAN. 14 Nov 2000. A Touchstone Book:
Published by Simon & Schuster

WORLD MYTHOLOGY. The Illustrated Guide.
General Editor: Roy Willis. Published by DBP (Duncan
Baird Publishers). London.

[1]   Some research from *The Secret History of the World* by Jonathan Black
      (Chapter 10, page, 179.)

[2]   See Jonathan Black, p. 180.

[3]   Note: Michael Faraday was the name of my spirit guide; although I
      cannot fathom why he would have been so interested in me, it seems
      important to my *id*, to at least mention Faraday's Cage, which was
      his invention and is used today in all Coaxial cable (TV cable). It is
      the surrounding and interwoven earth wire which protects the
      electrical signal within your TV Ariel cable and SCART lead
      (between Freeview box, DVD and TV) from any static interference.

ND - #0488 - 270225 - C0 - 229/152/18 - PB - 9781909544796 - Matt Lamination